ANALYZING DECISION MAKING

Metric Conjoint Analysis

JORDAN J. LOUVIERE
University of Alberta

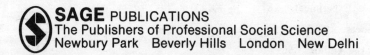

SAGE PUBLICATIONS
The Publishers of Professional Social Science
Newbury Park   Beverly Hills   London   New Delhi

CONTENTS

Acknowledgments   4

Series Editor's Introduction   5

Preface   7

1. Background Concepts and Theory   9

   1.0 Complex Decision Making and Conjoint
       Analysis   9

   1.1 A Theory of Complex Decision Making   12

   1.2 Algebraic Foundations of the Information
       Integration Theory Approach to Conjoint
       Analysis   14

   1.3 Comparison with Rank-Order Conjoint
       Methods   25

2. Design and Analysis of Conjoint Experiments   27

   2.0 Introduction   27

   2.1 The Design of Factorial Experiments   28

   2.2 Fractional Factorial Designs   35

   2.3 Analysis of Data from Factorial
       Conjoint Experiments   44

   2.4 Analysis of Individual Differences   47

**3. Practical Applications of Conjoint Theory
and Methods**   49

   3.0 Introduction   49

   3.1 Understanding the Decision Problem   50

   3.2 Identifying Determinant Attributes   50

   3.3 Developing Product Positioning Measures   52

   3.4 Practical Approaches to Solving Conjoint
       Problems   54

   3.5 Examples of Previous Applications of Conjoint
       Models to Practical Problems   63

**4. Predicting Likely Market Choices from
Conjoint Studies and Other Strategic
Applications of Conjoint Models**   67

   4.0 Introduction   67

   4.1 Approaches to Simulating Aggregate Market
       Choices Based on Conjoint Data or Individual
       Conjoint Models   68

   4.2 Integrating Conjoint and Discrete Choice
       Techniques to Study Choice Behavior
       Directly   76

   4.3 Concluding Remarks About Choice
       Experiments   87

References   89

About the Author   95

For information address:

SAGE Publications, Inc.
2111 West Hillcrest Drive
Newbury Park, California 91320

SAGE Publications Inc.   SAGE Publications Ltd.
275 South Beverly Drive   28 Banner Street
Beverly Hills   London EC1Y 8QE
California 90212   England

SAGE PUBLICATIONS India Pvt. Ltd.
M-32 Market
Greater Kailash I
New Delhi 110 048 India

International Standard Book Number 0-8039-2757-6

Library of Congress Catalog Card No. 87-072209

FIRST PRINTING

When citing a university paper, please use the proper form. Remember to cite the correct
Sage University Paper series title and include the paper number. One of the following
formats can be adapted (depending on the style manual used):

(1) IVERSEN, GUDMUND R. and NORPOTH, HELMUT (1976) "Analysis of Variance." Sage University Paper series on Quantitative Applications in the Social Sciences, 07-001. Beverly Hills: Sage Pubns.

OR

(2) Iversen, Gudmund R. and Norpoth, Helmut. 1976. *Analysis of Variance.* Sage University Paper series on Quantitative Applications in the Social Sciences, series no. 07-001. Beverly Hills: Sage Pubns.

ACKNOWLEDGMENTS

Many people contributed directly or indirectly to this manuscript. At the risk of omissions, let me first single out those who had an impact on my education, thinking, and research. I owe my interest and training in decision making to my graduate advisers Gerry Rushton, Don Dorfman, and Dave Reynolds. My thinking and research benefited from interactions with colleagues and co-researchers, particularly Irwin Levin, Ken Dueker, Lynn Beavers, Kent Norman, Moshe Ben-Akiva, Steve Lerman, Larry Ostresh, Dave Hensher, Les Johnson, Dave Curry, Joel Horowitz, and Harry Timmermans. A special debt is owed to Don Anderson and George Woodworth from whom I learned most of the statistics I now know. My graduate students also influenced me, especially Mike Piccolo, Bob Meyer, Tom Eagle, and Dave Henley.

The practical applications materials benefited considerably from interactions with and encouragement from a number of commercial firms and the assistance of government grants. I would like to give special thanks to David Evans, Tom Allen, John Aitchison, Eric Almquist, Steve Cohen, and Bill Jessiman for having enough faith in my work to take financial risks to develop commercial conjoint capabilities and to invest in research and development.

My wife, Cathy, unselfishly contributed her data management and computer skills to many, if not most, of my research efforts. Cathy also assisted with editing and organizing this manuscript, and compiled some of the references, tables, and figures.

Finally, Norman Anderson has encouraged my work in information integration theory since I was a Ph.D. student. This monograph would not have been possible without his encouragement and his many contributions to theory and methods in human judgment and decision making.

SERIES EDITOR'S INTRODUCTION

It is often assumed that individuals evaluate products and services by integrating salient attribute information about each. *Analyzing Decision Making*, by Jordan J. Louviere, describes how one can study and model such information integration processes and use the resulting models to forecast the choice behavior of the individuals studied or the populations they represent.

The monograph focuses upon "metric" conjoint methods. Metric conjoint methods are based on the assumption that individuals can evaluate multiattribute alternatives in such a way that their responses are approximately interval in measurement level. For example, the methods can be used to analyze data from judgment tasks in which individuals evaluate several multiattribute alternative on a category-rating scale. The attributes themselves are constructed according to statistical design principles such that the parameters of various decision models can be estimated.

The monograph concentrates on a general approach to estimating partial and joint evaluations or what are sometimes called *part-worth* utilities. This approach is known as functional measurement and is based on information integration theory, a theory of human information processing. The method by which one develops measures of partial evaluation components or partial utilities is called functional measurement because the partial measures of interest are those that "function" in models of human information processing.

Chapter 1 introduces the topic by discussing various algebraic decision models that describe alternate ways that consumers might process attribute information. A general model of attribute information processing is introduced (the multilinear model) that includes many other model forms (e.g., additive) as special cases. A comparison of metric with nonmetric methods is also provided.

In Chapter 2, the experimental bases for studying the model forms introduced in Chapter 1 are explained. Emphasis is placed on the design and analysis of factorial and fractional factorial experiments to implement conjoint research projects. Chapter 3 covers a broad range of practical application issues and also describes applications of metric conjoint methods in transport mode choice, recreation and shopping destination choice, residential choice, and other decisions.

Chapter 4 considers approaches to predicting the choices that individuals or groups of individuals are likely to make, based on their responses to conjoint experiments. Of central concern is how one develops conjoint models to forecast which one of several competing multi-attribute alternatives is likely to be chosen by each individual studied. A relatively new approach based on discrete dependent variable models is also described.

Conjoint analysis has so far been used chiefly by those seeking to explain consumer behavior in the marketplace. But there are numerous examples of how methods developed with one kind of behavior in mind generalize easily to other types of decisionmaking. We think that the publication of *Analyzing Decision Making* will add to this cross-disciplinary fertilization process.

—*Richard G. Niemi*
Series Co-Editor

PREFACE

Green and Wind (1973) published the first practical guide to modeling multiattribute judgments in marketing (see also Green and Rao, 1971). Since that time the academic and applied literature in conjoint analysis has grown enormously. For example, Slovic and Lichtenstein (1971), Slovic et al. (1977), Green and Srinivasan (1978) and Cattin and Wittink (1982, 1986) provide evidence that not only has the academic literature grown, but commercial applications of conjoint judgment and choice models also have increased substantially. Today a variety of paradigms, methods, and analytical techniques are commonly used in academic and commercial applications of conjoint analysis. For example, Cattin and Wittink (1982, 1986) report that commercial marketing researchers apply a number of different conjoint analysis approaches to solve practical problems in consumer decision making.

Unfortunately, the term "conjoint analysis," coined by Green and Srinivasan (1978) was implicitly defined to include any technique used to estimate attribute utilities based on subjects' responses to combinations of multiple decision attributes. This suggests that there is a general technique called conjoint analysis that one uses when one wants to model consumer decision making and develop measures of consumers' utilities. However, different "conjoint" paradigms have different assumptions, methods of analysis, and experimental procedures. Thus it is not only important to understand commonalities in conjoint paradigms, it is also important to understand differences.

This monograph is intended to be an introduction to theory and methods for studying customer decision processes. Information integration theory (IIT) (Anderson, 1981, 1982; Lynch, 1985; Louviere, 1974; 1984b; Bettman et al., 1975) provides the theoretical basis for the "how to" material in the applications chapters. Information integration theory is emphasized because it has a theoretical basis (Anderson, 1970, 1981, 1982) from which application methods logically follow and a well-developed error theory to support statistical tests of alternative models of consumer decision making.

Because IIT provides an excellent basis for understanding other conjoint analysis paradigms, this monograph does not review the field of human judgment and decision making or various other conjoint analysis paradigms of potential practical interest to marketing and related areas. Instead, it provides a relatively complete treatment of one approach, rather than an incomplete survey of a variety of approaches.

We assume that readers are familiar with the basics of analysis of variance and multiple linear regression models. In particular, the material in Chapters 1-3 relies heavily on these models, while Chapter 4 introduces concepts of discrete multivariate analysis. As a consequence, we do not review elementary statistical concepts because they can be found in many statistics texts.

Chapters 1 and 2 explain how to design conjoint analysis experiments and estimate statistical conjoint models in a manner consistent with IIT. Chapter 1 probably will interest academic researchers most, although the material in Chapter 1 is important to understand compromises required in applied work. Chapter 2 discusses the design of factorial and fractional factorial experiments to implement conjoint research studies. Chapter 3 focuses on using the theory in practical research settings, primarily based on application experiences with IIT in marketing, transportation planning, and related areas. Chapter 4 discusses approaches to forecasting consumer choice behavior, including an introduction to the design and analysis of discrete choice experiments based on IIT, discrete choice theory in econometrics, and discrete multivariate analysis in statistics.

Thus the objective of this monograph is to bring together information on theory and practical applications so that researchers who want to solve practical problems with a sound theoretical approach that has had considerable empirical success could find much of what they need in one volume.

ANALYZING DECISION MAKING
Metric Conjoint Analysis

JORDAN J. LOUVIERE
University of Alberta

1. BACKGROUND CONCEPTS AND THEORY

1.0 Complex Decision Making and Conjoint Analysis

The theory and methods of conjoint analysis discussed in this monograph deal with complex decision making, or the process of assessment, comparison, and/or evaluation in which consumers decide which aspects of products or services are important, compare products or services on each of the important aspects, and decide which one(s), if any, to choose. My orientation is influenced by the literature on information processing in judgment and decision making (see, e.g., Slovic and Lichtenstein, 1971; Slovic et al., 1977), although similar conceptualizations can be found elsewhere (see, e.g., Guilford, 1954; Lavidge and Steiner, 1961; McClelland, 1979).

The process of complex decision making is conceptualized in Figure 1.1. After acquiring information and learning about alternatives, consumers define a set of determinant attributes (Alpert, 1971) to use to compare and evaluate brands in a particular product class. After comparing available brands with respect to each of the attributes, consumers eliminate some alternatives and develop final "choice sets" of brands from which to choose (including the choice to delay or not purchase at all).

The process by which consumers compare brands on sets of determinant attributes, form final choice sets, and make choices is complicated. Figure 1.1 suggests that consumers form psychophysical as well as value judgments about brands. Psychophysical judgments (e.g., Gescheider, 1976) involve subjective perceptions of physical reality, in which indi-

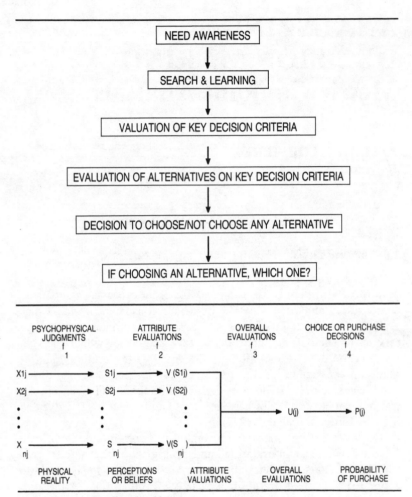

Figure 1.1 Complex Decision Making

viduals form impressions about the position of each considered brand with respect to each determinant attribute based on a number of physical brand characteristics. For example, if "convenience" is a determinant attribute of food stores, consumers might consider different physical factors, such as travel time, amount of parking space, hours of operation, parcel carryout, and check cashing, to form impressions of the "convenience" of particular stores.

Consumers probably do not perceive physical variables, such as travel time and amount of parking space, in physical measurement terms. Rather, they make psychophysical or perceptual judgments about each. Other factors, such as check cashing or parcel carryout, may be more accurately perceived because they can be more accurately observed. In any case, consumers form impressions or opinions about the positions of various brands on each determinant attribute that matters; and this process involves integrating perceptual information.

After consumers form impressions of the positions of various alternatives on the determinant attributes, they make value judgments about how good it is for alternatives to be so positioned on each attribute. This evaluation process can be inferred from an analysis of the way in which consumers combine (integrate) information about different determinant attributes to form overall impressions of brands. It is this integration or combining of attribute information that one studies with conjoint analysis techniques in general, and information integration theory (IIT) in particular.

Consumers' overall impressions, evaluations or judgments of the attributes of brands are relative to the set of brands that they consider. Hence it may change if (a) additional brands are added to those already evaluated, (b) new information is acquired that changes the set of determinant attributes by adding or deleting one or more (e.g., one learns that beers have different calorie levels; previously, all beers were thought to be the same), or (c) consumer beliefs about the values of attributes are changed by new information prior to choice (e.g., a friend says that her headaches are cured by extrastrength brand X with 750 mg. aspirin; previously brand X was thought to have only 500 mg.). Curry et al. (1983) and Lutz (1975), among others, discuss changes in consumer decision processes resulting from such alterations in cognitions.

Following the comparison, evaluation and impression-formation stage, consumers form final choice sets and decide which brand, if any, to choose. Commonly, this involves deciding which brand is better, taking into account all available information. Consumers then decide whether to purchase any of the brands, and if so, which one(s). If a consumer decides not to purchase, he or she may decide either to delay the purchase until a later time (e.g., wait for a sale) or to not purchase (e.g., "I can't afford this," or "This doesn't satisfy the need I had in mind"). The final choice is also a process that can be studied using conjoint analysis techniques, and is considered in Chapter 4.

The remainder of this chapter outlines algebraic theory that permits one to study these cognitive processes and develop statistical approximations to them, using conjoint analysis techniques. Subsequent chapters explain how to implement the theory and apply it in academic or practical settings.

1.1 A Theory of Complex Decision Making

The theory discussed in this section has been proposed by a number of different researchers in different fields. The version described here is derived primarily from the lens model developed by Egon Brunswick (reviewed, e.g., in Slovic and Lichtenstein, 1971), information integration theory developed by Anderson (e.g., 1970, 1981, 1982), and my own work (e.g., Louviere, 1974, 1979, 1982; Louviere and Meyer, 1981). Let us define a number of terms and concepts prior to the formal algebraic development in order that their meaning is clearly understood.

- The term *physical variable* refers to observations or measurements of various physical antecedents of determinant attributes that can be taken on real products.

- The term *attributes* is reserved for the determinant decision criteria consumers use to evaluate products or services.

- "Beliefs" that consumers have about the amount of each determinant attribute possessed by products or services are called the *positions* of each product on these attributes.

- Judgments that consumers make regarding "how good," "how satisfactory," or "how whatever" particular positions of particular products might be on particular determinant attributes are termed the consumers' *part-worth utilities*, or (*part-worths*) for the positions (levels) of those attributes.

- Judgments, impressions, or evaluations that consumers form of products or services, taking all the determinant attribute information into account (in a Gestalt sense) are called *overall evaluations*, or *overall utilities* for those products or services.

- The term *brand* means a particular product or service available in the market that can be evaluated and possibly selected by the consumer. That is, a brand refers to a possible product or service choice that a consumer might consider.

- A *final choice set* is the set of brands that a consumer seriously considers prior to making a choice. In marketing, this choice set often is called the *evoked set*.

- The term *choice* refers to the cognitive process by which a consumer, after evaluating all the brands and forming a final choice set, decides to select one of the brands or not to make a choice.

More formally, let X_{jk} represent a J × K array of physical variables (J represents the total number of brands; K the total number of determinant decision attributes) that underlie a consumer's attribute beliefs (positioning impressions). For simplicity we subscript X in two dimensions; however, each decision attribute may have multiple physical variable antecedents.

Let S_{jk} be an array of dimension J × K that constitutes the consumer's beliefs about the level of the k-th determinant decision attribute for the j-th brand of interest.

Let $V(S_{jk})$ be an array of dimension J × K that contains measures of the part-worth utilities of every element of S_{jk}; $V(S_{jk})$ therefore represents the consumer's opinions or feelings regarding the worth of the j-th brand's position on the k-th attribute.

Let U_j be a single dimensional array of dimension J × 1 representing a consumer's overall values or utilities for the j-th brand.

Let $p(j \mid A)$ represent a single dimensional array of dimension J × 1 that refers to the probability of selecting the j-th brand from a choice set A of (j = 1, 2, . . . , J) brands, of which j is a member; $p(j \mid A)$ is defined over all elements of A (brands in A).

These formal definitions allow us to outline the relationships that we assume to operate in complex decision making. These relationships may be expressed as follows:

$$S_{jk} = f1_k(X_{jk}), \quad (k = 1, 2, \ldots, K; \; j = 1, 2, \ldots, J), \qquad [1.1]$$

$$V(S_{jk}) = f2_k(S_{jk}), \qquad [1.2]$$

$$U_j = f3[V(S_{jk})], \qquad [1.3]$$

$$p(j \mid A) = f4(U_j), \qquad [1.4]$$

where

X_{jk} is the k-th physical variable measure(s) for the j-th brand.

S_{jk} is the k-th belief measure about the "position" of the j-th brand on the k-th attribute.

$V(S_{jk})$ is the k-th part-worth utility measure associated with the k-th position measure of the j-th brand.

U_j is the overall value or utility to measure of the j-th brand.

$p(j|A)$ is the probability of choosing the j-th brand from choice set A, of which j is a member.

$f1_k, f2_k, f3, f4$ are mappings.

By elementary substitution, we derive:

$$p(j|A) = f4\{f3[f2_k(f1_k(X_{kj}))]\}, \quad \text{or,} \qquad [1.5]$$

$$p(j|A) = F(X_{jk}), \qquad [1.6]$$

where F is a composite function of the indicated mappings in Equation 1.5.

Equation 1.5 states that the probability of choosing brand j from choice set A is a function of observable measures of reality corresponding to each of the K determinant decision attributes. This composite function indicates that several different levels of explanation of choice behavior are possible: (a) explanations based entirely on physical variables, (b) explanations based only on belief (or positioning) variables, (c) explanations using only part-worths, and/or (d) explanations containing combinations of these variables. This monograph focuses on the use of psychological variables to explain consumer judgment and choice behavior, although economic approaches to the study of decision making and choice behavior are also accommodated by equation 1.6 (e.g., Hensher and Johnson, 1980; Manski and McFadden, 1981; Ben-Akiva and Lerman, 1985).

1.2 Algebraic Foundations of the Information Integration Theory Approach to Conjoint Analysis

1.2.1 A BRIEF OVERVIEW OF INFORMATION INTEGRATION THEORY

Information integration theory (IIT) was developed by Norman H. Anderson (see, e.g., Anderson, 1981, 1982). It is a theory about the behavior of numerical data in response to multiple pieces of information. The numerical data of interest consist of individual or group category-rating responses to combinations of different decision variables (attributes). Complex decision making involves searching for, acquiring, and processing information; hence one can use IIT to study information processing revealed by consumers' responses to multi-attribute options. IIT is similar in conceptual orientation to social Judgment Theory (Adelman et al., 1974) and bears a strong resemblance in experimental format to axiomatic conjoint measurement (see Section 1.3). These latter two paradigms also allow one to develop conjoint models of individual decision processes, however their theoretical and methodological bases differ from one another and from IIT.

IIT can also be used to study risky decision making (see, e.g., Lopes, 1986) and, thus, has much in common with axiomatic utility theory in economics, management science, and statistics (e.g., Keeney and Raiffa, 1976). Of these paradigms, only IIT possesses a theory of errors (except for certain special cases, e.g., Eliashberg and Hauser, 1985). Error theories are important because they permit one to falsify models. Unfortunately, most commonly used conjoint techniques do not permit models to be falsified (e.g., MONANOVA).

Let us now consider the basic assumptions of information integration theory:

(1) The unknown and unobservable overall utility that a consumer has in his or her mind regarding the j-th brand is linearly related to a consumer's response on a category-rating scale. That is,

$$U_j = a + bR_j + e_j,$$

where U is as previously defined, R(j) is the observed response on a category-rating scale, and e(j) is a normally distributed error term with zero expectation and constant variance, which satisfies assumptions of analysis of variance or multiple regression.

(2) The category-ranking scale used by a consumer under appropriate experimental instructions and task conditions approximates an interval measurement level.

(3) A consumer's response strategy reveals his or her decision strategy. The response strategy can be approximated by algebraic conjoint models amenable to experimental investigation and statistical parameterization.

Assumption 2 may be relaxed through the use of alternative response modes, such as binary (yes/no) scales or multiple choice scales (which one of the following discrete response categories is the "best," "highest," "most preferred," and so on), as explained in Chapter 4. Moreover, IIT permits the use of monotone transformations to remove response scale nonlinearities that might make categorical responses of subjects ordinal and not interval in measurement level. However, only once has such rescaling been required in empirical applications (see Anderson, 1981, 1982).

The measurement level of category-rating scales is a controversial issue, illustrated by the debate between Anderson and Krantz and Tversky in the early 1970s (see, Anderson, 1971; Krantz and Tversky, 1971b). However, it seems to be more acceptable to assume that under appropriate experimental instructions and task conditions, subjects can and do use category-rating scales in an approximately equal interval manner. Regardless of one's beliefs about the measurement level of judgments made by individuals on category-rating scales, such scales form an intimate and important link in the logic chain of IIT. Thus let us turn our attention to the algebraic and statistical theory of IIT.

1.2.2 ALGEBRAIC AND STATISTICAL FORMALITIES

IIT posits that simple algebraic conjoint models are valid approximations to the unknown and unobservable judgment and decision processes of consumers. All models discussed in this section describe a subject's judgment or decision responses "as if" a consumer uses the valuation and integration rules (or decision heuristics) implied by the algebraic form of his or her conjoint model. The process that subjects "really use" is presently unknowable.

With that caveat in mind, let us discuss a very simple conjoint model—an adding model. Adding models are widely assumed in applications of conjoint analysis. That is, they are the most often assumed mapping for equation 1.3 (see, e.g., Green and Rao, 1971; Green and Srinivasan, 1978). The adding model can be written as follows for three determinant attributes:

$$U_j = C + V(S_{1j}) + V(S_{2j}) + V(S_{3j}), \qquad [1.8]$$

where C is an additive constant, necessary to set a zero point on an interval scale, and $V(S_{1j}) - V(S_{3j})$ are part-worth utilities for the three attributes of the j-th brand.

We assume that $V(S_{1j}) - V(S_{3j})$ represent a consumer's unknown part-worths for three determinant attributes. Each level of each attribute may have a different part-worth utility. Different brands can be described by combinations of different attribute levels; hence each combination represents a different brand. Additive decision processes imply that consumers add the separate part-worth utilities to evaluate each brand.

For example, decisions about public bus transportation options might involve attributes such as fare, travel time to and from destinations, and walking distance. An almost infinite array of different buses (brands) can be created by combining various numerical values of fare, travel time, and walking distance. Thus $V(S_{1j})$ can be assigned different values, as can $V(S_{2j})$ and $V(S_{3j})$. Henceforth we refer to such attribute values as *levels* to avoid confusion with our use of the term *values* (or *part-worth utilities*: see Section 1.1); and also because the term levels is used in the experimental design literature discussed in Chapter 3. Let us denote the levels of attributes 1-3 as S_{1p}, S_{2q} and S_{3r}; and the corresponding part-worth utilities, as $V(S_{1p})$, $V(S_{2q})$ and $V(S_{3r})$. Thus each p-th, q-th, r-th combination of levels represents one brand.

Thus instead of writing U_j, we will write U_{pqr} with no loss of generality, but it will mean U_j. The total number of brands that one can create for a particular conjoint analysis problem is the product of the p, q, and r levels. The total number of possible brands is therefore a combinatorial problem defined by the set of possible combinations of the levels p, q, and r. Such problems are called "factorial" problems, and there is an extensive literature in statistics concerned with their treatment. In particular, such problems arise in the design of factorial experiments discussed in Chapter 2 (e.g., Winer, 1971), which are the experimental vehicles used to implement IIT in practical problem situations.

IIT is concerned with developing and testing algebraic conjoint models of individuals' responses to factorial arrays of brands described by different combinations of levels of sets of determinant attributes. Consumers evaluate $p \times q \times r \times \ldots \times z$ combinations of attribute levels on category-rating scales; each combination of levels of the determinant attributes represents a unique "brand" or choice alternative. Figure 1.2 provides an example of a set of determinant attribute combinations for public buses. The attributes are fare, travel time, and distance to the nearest bus stop; each attribute has two levels.

Let us now return to the additive decision model (equation 1.8), rewriting it for a single consumer as follows:

$$U_{pqr} = C + V(S_{1p}) + V(S_{2q}) + V(S_{3r}), \qquad [1.9]$$

where all terms were defined previously.

Recall that we cannot observe U_{pqr}. Rather, we observe a consumer's

Experimental Attributes

A Subject's Average Ratings (2 repl'ns.)	Bus Fare ($)	Travel Time (in minutes)	Walking Distance (in blocks)
18.57	0.50	30	1
8.29	0.50	30	6
6.14	0.50	60	1
3.57	0.50	60	6
11.94	1.50	30	1
5.77	1.50	30	6
4.49	1.50	60	1
2.94	1.50	60	6

OLS Estimates: Marginal and Interaction Means

Means	Fare ($)	Time (in minutes)	Distance (in blocks)
9.14	0.50		
6.29	1.50		
11.14		30	
4.29		60	
10.29			1
5.14			6
13.43	0.50	30	
4.86	0.50	60	
8.86	1.50	30	
3.72	1.50	60	
12.36	0.50		1
5.93	0.50		6
8.22	1.50		1
4.36	1.50		6
15.26		30	1
7.03		30	6
5.32		60	1
3.26		60	6

Figure 1.2: An Example Factorial Design: Combinations of Levels of Fare, Travel Time, and Walking Distance to Bus Stop

evaluations, R_{pqr}, on a category-rating scale. Substituting Equation 1.7 and transposing, we have:

$$R_{pqr} = C + V(S_{1p}) + V(S_{2q}) + V(S_{3r}) + e_{pqr}, \qquad [1.10]$$

where all terms were defined previously. Equation 1.10 suggests that a consumer's ratings are an additive function of the "true" but unknown part-worth utilities (the $V(S_k)$'s). The error assumptions of IIT imply that analysis of variance or multiple linear regression can be used as the error theory to test the additive decision hypothesis of equation 1.9.

If a consumer evaluates each of the $p \times q \times r$ combinations more than once, there are sufficient observations to test equation 1.9. If equation 1.10 (the empirical realization of equation 1.9) is true, there will be no nonadditivities in a consumer's response data. That is, only the purely additive terms will be nonzero in a statistical analysis—there will be no significant interaction effects in an analysis of variance or multiple linear regression analysis if equation 1.9 is true. This conclusion can be proved by deducing what happens if we subtract the response to level 2 of attribute 1 from the response to level 1 of attribute 1, holding other attributes constant:

$$R_{1qr} - R_{2qr} = [C + V(S_{11}) + V(S_{2q}) + V(S_{3r}) + e_{1qr}] \qquad [1.11]$$

$$- [C + V(S_{12}) + V(S_{2q}) + V(S_{3r}) + e_{2qr}],$$

$$= V(S_{11}) - V(S_{12}) + (e_{1qr} - e_{2qr}).$$

All terms were defined previously. Equation 1.11 indicates that the difference in the part-worth utilities of levels 1 and 2 of attribute 1 is a constant; hence, curves of response data for each level of attribute 1 graphed against levels of attribute 2 (or 3) must be parallel. Responses to levels of one attribute are *independent* of responses to levels of other attributes, a property that generalizes to any number of attributes.

Thus, if the decision process revealed by a consumer's rating behavior is additive, we expect to retain the null hypothesis of no interaction effects in an analysis of variance or multiple linear regression analysis. Hence, the additive decision process hypothesis can be falsified by using analysis of variance or multiple linear regression to test the main and interaction effects of consumers' ratings data. However, consumers must rate each brand (combination of attribute levels) at least twice in order to have enough degrees of freedom to perform the necessary statistical tests. If an experimental (factorial) design is small (for example, a $2 \times 2 \times 2$), multiple replications are little problem. However, as the size of an experiment grows, by increasing the number of attribute levels, by increasing the number of attributes, or by both, it becomes impractical to ask consumers to rate multiple replications in field research. Hence one must find other ways to attack the problem, some of which are discussed in Chapters 3 and 4, although a complete diagnosis (test) of any hypothesized conjoint model requires replicated factorial experiments.

Each complete set of ratings of attribute combinations is termed a *replication*. Combinations of attribute levels are called *treatments*, or *treatment combinations*. These terms will be used throughout the remainder of the monograph. Conjoint experiments in which consumers evaluate treatments more than once are termed *repeated measures* experiments. Repeated measures experiments require special care in analysis, because consumers' responses cannot be assumed to be independent. In a repeated measures problem, each term in an analysis of variance or multiple linear regression model has a separate error component. It is incorrect to "lump" all the within- and between-replication effects into residual mean square (error). Rather, the appropriate statistical test of the significance of each effect in a replicated conjoint experiment is a test of the variability in that effect from replication to replication. Little variability implies high precision and significance.

One must be cautious, however, because interaction effects may be close to zero and quite precisely estimated. Spurious effects may manifest themselves as significant interactions in an error analysis. To avoid mistaking spurious interactions for real, it is wise to (a) examine the magnitude of the estimated parameter if multiple linear regression is used to make the test and/or (b) plot the data to see if the response curves are parallel.

Let us now turn our attention to estimating the part-worth utilities—the $V(S_{1p})$, $V(S_{2q})$ and $V(S_{3r})$. Rewriting equation 1.10 for convenience, we have:

$$R_{pqr} = C + V(S_{1p}) + V(S_{2q}) + V(S_{3r}) + e_{pqr}. \qquad [1.12]$$

Consider the result of averaging equation 1.12 over attributes 2 and 3 (or subscripts q and r):

$$R_{p..} = C + V(S_{1p}) + V(S_{2.}) + V(S_{3.}) + e_{p..}, \qquad [1.13]$$

$$= [C + V(S_{2.}) + V(S_{3.})] + V(S_{1p}) + e_{p..},$$

where dots (.) refer to the effects of averaging. Equation 1.13 constitutes a theorem that states that the marginal means ($R_{p.}$) of a consumer's response data are equal to the unknown part-worth utilities ($V(S_k)$'s) up to a linear transformation. That is, the marginal response means are interval scale measures of the unknown part-worth utilities because a linear transformation is the only permissible transformation for interval scales (see, e.g., Figure 1.2).

This last conclusion, of course, is true only if an additive model is "correct." Thus, if an additive model passes the statistical tests described earlier, one can use the marginal response means to represent the consumer's part-worth utilities for each level of each determinant attribute. Further, the $V(S_k)$'s must be a function of the S_k's; hence one can specify equation 1.2 by graphing the marginal means against the experimental S_k levels: the k-th graph of $V(S_k)$ versus S_k is an estimate of the k-th mapping in equation 1.2. The process of using a conjoint model to estimate the unknown scale values from the respondent's rating data is called functional measurement (Anderson, 1970). The term *functional measurement* refers to the fact that the theoretically correct estimates of the part-worth utilities are those that "function" in a conjoint model.

Thus one can test additive conjoint models and, if they cannot be rejected, one can infer relationships between beliefs and part-worth utilities (equation 1.2). Fortunately, this conclusion is a fairly general one: One can use this logic to develop and test other algebraic conjoint models, one can derive estimates of the unknown part-worth utilities, and one can approximate equation 1.2 for individual consumers and groups of consumers (segments).

1.2.3 OTHER ALGEBRAIC CONJOINT MODELS OF POSSIBLE INTEREST

Numerous other model possibilities exist, but we will confine our attention to the most common specific and general forms represented by the class of algebraic conjoint models know as simple polynomials (Krantz and Tversky, 1971a). The class of simple polynomials includes additive, multiplicative, distributive, and dual-distributive models of the mapping in equation 1.3. The multilinear model is the general form for these simple polynomials, and it can be written as follows for three determinant attributes:

$$U_{pqr} = C_0 + C_1 V(S_{1p}) + C_2 V(S_{2q}) + C_3 V(S_{3r}) \qquad [1.14]$$

$$+ C_4 V(S_{1p}) V(S_{2q}) + C_5 V(S_{1p}) V(S_{3r})$$

$$+ C_6 V(S_{2q}) V(S_{3r}) + C_7 V(S_{1p}) V(S_{2q}) V(S_{3r}),$$

where the C_0 is the origin of the utility scale and C_{1-7} are scaling constants. Equation 1.14 implies that attributes can be complements, substitutes, or independent. The multilinear form allows a general approach to studying decision processes, because it accommodates completely multiplicative processes (all attributes are complements); distributive processes (one attribute complements the other two, which are jointly independent); and dual-distributive processes (one attribute is independent of two others that are complements). These models can be specified as follows:

$$U_{pqr} = C_0 + C_1 [V(S_{1p}) V(S_{2q}) V(S_{3r})], \text{ [multiplicative]} \qquad [1.15]$$

$$U_{pqr} = C_0 + C_1 V(S_{1p}) [V(S_{2q}) + V(S_{3r})], \text{ [distributive]} \qquad [1.16]$$

$$U_{pqr} = C_0 + C_1 V(S_{1p}) + C_2 V(S_{2q}) V(S_{3r}), \text{ [dual-distributive]} \qquad [1.17]$$

where all terms have been defined previously.

Equations 1.15-1.17 are subsets of the multilinear form in which one or more C terms are equal to zero. Thus the multilinear form can be used as the general form for estimation and testing: all results that apply to this form also apply to equations 1.15-1.17. Let us now consider the result of subtracting the second level of attribute 1 from the first level of attribute 1 for the multilinear conjoint model as we did with equation 1.11:

$$R_{1qr} - R_{2qr} = [C_0 + C_1 V(S_{11}) + C_2 V(S_{2q}) + C_3 V(S_{3r}) \qquad [1.18]$$

$$+ C_4 V(S_{11}) V(S_{2q}) + C_5 V(S_{11}) V(S_{3r})$$

$$+ C_6 V(S_{2q}) V(S_{3r})$$

$$+ C_7 V(S_{11}) V(S_{2q}) V(S_{3r}) + e_{1qr}]$$

$$- [C_0 + C_1 V(S_{12}) + C_2 V(S_{2q}) + C_3 V(S_{3r})$$

$$+ C_4 V(S_{12}) V(S_{2q}) + C_5 V(S_{12}) V(S_{3r})$$

$$+ C_6 V(S_{2q}) V(S_{3r})$$

$$+ C_7 V(S_{12}) V(S_{2q}) V(S_{3r}) + e_{2qr}]$$

$$= C_1 [V(S_{11} - V(S_{12})] + C_4 V(S_{2q}) [V(S_{11})$$

$$- V(S_{12})] + C_5 V(S_{3r}) [V(S_{11}) - V(S_{12})]$$

$$+ C_7 V(S_{2q}) V(S_{3r}) [V(S_{11} - V(S_{12})]$$

$$+ (e_{1qr} - e_{2qr}),$$

where all terms are as previously defined; however, the Cs are now collected constants defined by the substitution of equation 1.7 into equation 1.14. Equation 1.18 indicates that the shape of the curves for levels of $V(S_1)$ graphed as a function of $V(S_2)$, $V(S_3)$, or both $V(S_2)$ and $V(S_3)$, depend upon which C coefficients are significantly different from zero. Hence the relationships in equation 1.18 are determined by the interaction coefficients for the terms in $V(S_{1p})$, (C_4, C_5 and C_7), confirming that the multilinear form includes the other simple polynomials as a special case.

One can demonstrate that the marginal response means of a multilinear conjoint model are interval scale estimates of the unknown $V(S_{kx})$ parameters by using the derivation procedure that produced equation 1.18. However, in the interests of brevity, we shall not derive the theorem, but merely state it: Marginal response means from a factorial experimental design constitute an interval scale estimate of the unknown part-worth utilities of each attribute if some subset of the multilinear model form is correct.

This result for the marginal means also holds for any set of regression coefficients that represent these means, because the p-th, q-th, and r-th marginal means can be described exactly by polynomials of degree p-1, q-1, and r-1, respectively. In practice, orthogonal polynomial codes (see Section 2.2.1), dummy codes, or effects codes are used to estimate marginal means in regression models. Hence regression coefficients that represent the marginal means are also interval scales of the part-worths.

In the case of the multilinear model, the pattern of nonzero C values uniquely diagnoses various subset models. In particular, if $C_1 - C_7$ are all nonzero and positive in sign (equation 1.15), the multiplicative form is supported. To prove this, recall that the k-th marginal means are linearly related to the unknown $V(S_k)$'s. For example, in the case of $V(S_{1p})$:

$$V(S_{1p}) = a_1 + a_2 R_{p..} + e_{p..}, \qquad [1.19]$$

where all terms have been defined previously. Transpose $R_{p..}$ to the left-hand side; form another linear relationship, substitute this relationship for $V(S_{1p})$ in equation 1.15, and repeat this for $V(S_{2q})$ and $V(S_{3r})$. The resulting equation is multilinear in the Rs. Similarly, substituting transposed equation 1.19 into equations 1.16 and 1.17 yields subsets of the multilinear model corresponding to distribution and dual distribution, respectively. This result permits diagnosis or testing of conjoint models.

In particular, if any subset of a general multilinear conjoint model is correct, the pattern of significance (nonsignificance) of the terms in an analysis of variance or multiple linear regression analysis of a consumer's response data uniquely diagnoses (tests) an unknown (hypothesized) conjoint model. Thus, as discussed earlier, analysis of variance or multiple linear regression models serve as an error theory to test various hypothesized algebraic conjoint models of interest.

Hence, if one assumes that a consumer's responses to combinations of levels of attributes on category-rating scales for some response dimension of interest (e.g., preference) are approximately interval in measurement level, one can demonstrate the following:

(1) Repeated responses to a complete factorial enumeration of combinations of levels of attributes provide sufficient error variability to uniquely diagnose (test) various conjoint model forms (equation 1.3) that describe how consumers evaluate brands.

(2) If a consumer's decision process can be approximated by a multilinear conjoint model, one can obtain interval scale estimates of the unknown "part-worth utilities" by calculating the marginal means of the respondent's data, or the corresponding regression coefficients.

(3) One can relate the part-worth estimates $(V(S_k))$ to the corresponding S_k's (the levels of the attributes used in the experiment). These relationships represent empirical estimates of equation 1.2 for each consumer.

(4) If the attribute levels used in the experiment are levels of physical variables, one can approximate equation 1.1. However, if the attributes are not physical variables, one must independently study the relationship between the positioning measures (beliefs) and the corresponding physical variables.

1.3 Comparison with Rank-Order Conjoint Methods

As originally discussed by Green and Wind (1973) and as subsequently used by many researchers, "conjoint analysis" studies often rely on tasks in which subjects rank-order different brands (1 to J) described by combinations of levels of different determinant attributes. The rank-orderings can be analyzed to derive estimates of the part-worth utilities for each level of each attribute, assuming that certain kinds of simple polynomial conjoint models are correct. The theory underlying this approach to modeling decision making is termed *axiomatic conjoint measurement* (Luce and Tukey, 1964; Tversky, 1967; Krantz and Tversky, 1971a; Krantz et al., 1972; Barron, 1977). Thus, if certain axiomatic conditions are satisfied in real rank-orderings, the rankings can be represented as if they were generated by various conjoint model forms (e.g., additive model forms).

In addition, it also can be demonstrated that if the axioms are satisfied, part-worth utilities can be measured on scales that are asymptotically interval in measurement level. *Asymptotically interval* means that if there is a sufficiently dense spacing of the levels of the attributes and the axioms are satisfied, the derived part-worth utilities become closer to interval-level measures as the spacing density increases. If subjects can rank-order attribute combinations, theory exists to determine which of a number of algebraic conjoint models most closely represents their rankings.

Unfortunately, rankings of real subjects rarely satisfy all of the axioms necessary to diagnose an "appropriate" algebraic conjoint model. Without a theory about the way that errors behave in real rankings, one does not know how many violations of a given set of axioms is too many or whether systematic patterns of violations indicate one model or another. Lacking an error theory, therefore, one is forced to make assumptions about the appropriate algebraic form of a conjoint model. Almost all published academic and applied studies have assumed additive conjoint models to be appropriate, although nonadditive model forms could have been accommodated (e.g., Green and Wind, 1973).

Practical, rank-order conjoint analysis relies on certain computer algorithms to derive point estimates of part-worth utilities. Commonly, MONANOVA (Kruskal, 1965) is used to estimate part-worth utilities assuming an additive conjoint model to be appropriate. MONANOVA is an acronym for MONotonic ANalysis Of VAriance, and involves the use of an iterative algorithm to find estimates of attribute part-worths such that the rank order of their sum for each combination of attribute levels is correlated as closely as possible to that combination's observed rank order.

Comparisons of estimates obtained from MONANOVA with OLS estimates obtained by regressing the ranks against a matrix of dummy codes representing the attribute levels varied in the conjoint experiment suggest that both methods produce nearly identical results (see Green and Srinivasan, 1978). Unfortunately, OLS normally cannot be used to estimate interaction effects from ranking data if additive models are inappropriate. Rather, point estimates of interaction effects can be obtained from algorithms like PREFMAP (Green and Wind, 1973; Green and Devita, 1974; Green and Srinivasan, 1978).

Indeed, many nonmetric (rank-order) scaling methods rely on badness-of-fit indices called "stress" to decide on the adequacy of estimated models. As demonstrated by Dawes and Corrigan (1974), Anderson and Shanteau (1977), and others, if certain monotonic conditions are satisfied, additive models almost always will produce very high R-square values, even when wrong. Because of the similarity of stress to the R-square measures used in regression analysis, it is very likely that this problem also extends to rank-order conjoint methods. Thus researchers should be cautious about using stress values to determine the adequacy of models' fit to ranking data.

Somewhat more bothersome, however, is the philosophical problem of the degree of scientific generalization possible from parameter estimation methods that permit any monotone transformation of the response data, so long as the data are ordinally consistent with a hypothesized conjoint model form. Thus, if an analyst does not know which monotone transformation of the data is used by the algorithm, and this transformation is different for different individuals, it raises questions about scientific generalizability. Moreover, this practice is inconsistent with a view of science as trying to develop laws and regularities for particular measurement systems.

The major advantage of rank-order methods is that one does not have to assume that subjects use rating scales in an equal interval manner. Rather, one can make the weaker assumption of ordinality. It is also sometimes argued that subjects find it easier to rank-order sets of attribute combinations than to rate them on rating scales (see, e.g., Green and Srinivasan, 1978: 112). This argument has no empirical basis, and many argue the reverse, namely, that subjects find it easier to rate than rank. It also is not obvious what the word "easier" means, and thus this argument is unlikely to have a clear resolution.

Because it has an error theory that permits one to test competing models and to estimate part-worth utilities, IIT is a comprehensive theory of the behavior of response data for the types of conjoint experiments explained in this monograph. Reliance on analysis of variance and multiple linear regression methods with which many are likely to be familiar is an additional advantage. IIT also provides a basis for developing the tests of competing models and estimates of part-worths in Chapter 4, which deals with the design and analysis of discrete response data, focusing on choice data. Thus a single paradigm can be used to explain basic concepts in conjoint analysis and to discuss extensions of discrete response tasks in which subjects make choices among competing options. This should provide a good foundation for studying rank-order methods should one be so inclined.

The next chapter deals with the design and analysis of factorial and fractional factorial conjoint analysis experiments that are necessary to implement the theory discussed in this chapter.

2. DESIGN AND ANALYSIS OF CONJOINT EXPERIMENTS

2.0 Introduction

The theory of information integration in judgment and decision making that underlies the conjoint methods explained in this monograph was outlined in Chapter 1. Implementation of concepts from Chapter 1 is explained by discussing both the design and analysis of conjoint experiments. We first describe the design and analysis of factorial conjoint experiments and then explain the design of fractional factorial conjoint experiments. Following the discussion of design principles, we explain how to analyze conjoint data with analysis of variance and/or multiple linear regression. The chapter concludes with the analysis of individual differences.

2.1 The Design of Factorial Experiments

As explained in the previous chapter, factorial designs involve combinations of levels of decision attributes. In the experimental design literature, decision attributes are termed "factors," and the values that each attribute take on or are assigned in an experiment are called "levels." Experimental factors and their levels are completely under the control of the experimenter; and one is free to choose whatever factors and levels are of interest. The choice of factors and levels, therefore, is dictated by a particular decision problem (see, e.g., Snedecor and Cochran, 1974; Winer, 1971).

In Chapter 3 we discuss identification of appropriate determinant attributes (factors) to use in conjoint experiments and how to choose levels for these attributes. In this chapter we assume that one has determined the attributes and levels and wants to design and analyze a conjoint experiment using these attributes. We also assume elementary knowledge of experimental design, and we emphasize the design and analysis of fractional factorial experiments because of their value in practical work. Some reference to basic design theory, however, is necessary, and where such reference is made we shall note textbooks in which further information can be found.

2.1.1 TWO-ATTRIBUTE (FACTOR) DESIGNS

The two-factor case serves as an introduction to the problem and as a basis for a discussion of important concepts and issues that arise in larger problems. We adhere to the previous notation established in Chapter 1, recalling that interest centers on responses made by consumers on category-rating scales. The problem, therefore, is to diagnose (if we lack an a priori hypothesis) or test (if we have an a priori hypothesis) an appropriate decision model for a consumer who evaluates combinations of levels of two determinant attributes on a category-rating scale. Let us consider three possible models for this problem (although there are other possibilities):

$$U_{pq} = C_0 + C_1 V(S_{1p}) + C_2 V(S_{2q}),$$ [2.1]

$$U_{pq} = C_0 + C_1 V(S_{1p}) V(S_{2q}),$$ [2.2]

$$U_{pq} = C_0 + C_1 V(S_{1p}) + C_2 V(S_{2q}) + C_3 V(S_{1p}) V(S_{2q}),$$ [2.3]

where all terms are as defined in Chapter 1.

Equation 2.1 is an additive model, with scaling constants $C_0 - C_2$; equation 2.2 is a multiplicative model with scaling constants C_0 and C_1; and equation 2.3 is a multilinear model with scaling constants $C_0 - C_3$. Chapter 1 proved that marginal means are interval scale estimates of the unknown $V(S_k)$ parameters, if a subset of the multilinear model is correct. Diagnosis (testing) of equations 2.1-2.3 requires use of at least three levels for each attribute because with only two levels, the marginal means trivially satisfy the linearity conditions implied by the equations (see Figure 2.1 in Section 2.1.2 below).

Thus, in principle, three levels of each attribute are required to correctly diagnose (test) conjoint models. If an attribute has two levels, the linearity conditions implied by equation 2.1 are satisfied, but not necessarily the additivity conditions. Thus two levels are sufficient to reject additivity, but not to fully test a model. Let us therefore consider a two-attribute experiment in which both attributes have three levels: the levels of attribute S_1 are denoted p1, p2, and p3, and the levels of attribute S_2 are q1, q2, and q3. This experiment has nine combinations of levels: p1q1, p1q2, p1q3, p2q1, p2q2, p2q3, p3q1, p3q2, and p3q3. A consumer rates each of the nine combinations of levels on a category-rating scale; and we represent these rating responses as follows: R(p1q1), R(p1q2), R(p1q3), . . . , R(p3q3).

As noted in Chapter 1, these ratings are uncertain estimates of the true, but unknown, overall utilities, or U_{pq}. We can represent the variation in these estimates as follows:

Total Variation in R_{pq} = Variation due to S_{1p}

+ Variation due to S_{2q}

+ Variation due to both S_{1p} & S_{2q}

+ Variation due to random error.

These variance components can be decomposed separately only if a consumer evaluates each of the nine combinations of levels at least twice, or if we have a priori information that some one or more of the components (or pieces of the components) are equal to zero. This is because the variation can be partitioned as follows:

S_1 has three levels, and therefore two degrees of freedom (can be partitioned into two independent sources of variation).

S_2 has three levels, and therefore two degrees of freedom (can be partitioned into two independent sources of variation).

S_1 & S_2 have four interaction degrees of freedom (can be partitioned into four independent sources of vatiation).

There are therefore eight degrees of freedom to be accounted for by nine attribute-level combinations, plus an additional degree of freedom for the grand mean. Thus no statistical tests can be conducted on the response data if a consumer rates the combinations only once because the statistical model is "saturated"; that is, all available degrees of freedom are used to estimate the parameters, leaving none for error.

2.1.2 A NOTE ABOUT REPEATED MEASURES DESIGNS

In the classical case of a two-factor experiment, unique observations (i.e., one rating by one consumer) are randomly assigned to each combination of levels of the experimental factors. This sampling scheme satisfies the independence conditions of analysis of variance or multiple linear regression, but cannot be used to understand individual decision making. To model the decision process of an individual consumer or a group of homogeneous consumers (a market segment) requires more than one response from the same consumer(s) to each combination of attribute levels. Such experiments are termed "repeated measures" designs, or sometimes, "within- (and between-) subjects" designs. Such designs pose special analytical problems because responses to each replication are not independent.

Repeated measures designs are fundamental to the correct implementation of IIT, hence we must consider their analysis. Let us rewrite the consumer's response as R_{ipq} (i indexes replications). The components of variation may now be expressed as:

Variation in R_{ipq} due to S_{1p}

Variation in R_{ipq} due to S_{2q}

Variation in R_{ipq} due to $S1p$ and S_{2q}

Variation in R_{ipq} due to replication variation in S_{1p}

Variation in R_{ipq} due to replication variation in S_{21}

Variation in R_{ipq} due to replication variation in S_{1p} and S_{2q}.

Ordinarily we require a measure of pure error to test each component separately; and these measures of pure error are given by the replication-to-replication variation in each main and interaction effect: that is, S_{1p}, S_{2q} and $S_{1p}S_{2q}$. These effects are normally tested as follows:

(1) Equation 2.1 is tested by means of the two-way interaction between S_{1p} and S_{2q}. This effect is tested against its interaction with the replications factor, which measures replication-to-replication variability in that effect. One tests if this variability is sufficiently large to retain the null hypothesis. Retention of the null hypothesis is evidence in favor of equation 2.1, while rejection of the null hypothesis of no significant interaction effect invalidates equation 2.1. If the interaction is not significant, one can estimate the part-worth utilities by calculating the marginal means, or their regression counterparts.

Estimates of the part-worth utilities (the $V(S_k)$'s) can be used to predict a subject's observed data, and residuals from prediction can be analyzed with analysis of variance or multiple linear regression to test whether the nonlinear components of the effects are statistically significant. If significant, this invalidates an additive model, possibly suggesting that the way in which the subject used the rating scale did not satisfy the interval-measurement-level assumptions. Nonsignificance of the nonlinear components of the effects supports the additive model of equation 2.1.

(2) If the two-way interaction is significant, and equation 2.2 or 2.3 is correct, one can use the marginal means or their regression counterparts to estimate the part-worths. These estimates can be used in equations 2.2 or 2.3 to predict a subject's responses. As before, residuals from prediction can be analyzed by analysis of variance or multiple regression to test the null hypothesis of no significant effects. Lack of significance supports a particular model form, while significance signals a rejection, or at least a warning that response scale nonlinearity may be a problem.

(3) The multiplying model of equation 2.2 may be distinguished from the more general model of 2.3 by using multiple linear regression analysis to estimate the parameters of the two-way interaction component using the marginal means and their cross-products in orthogonal form as the independent predictors (see Sections 2.2.1 and 3.2.1.6 for a

discussion of orthogonal polynomials). If a multiplying model is correct, the coefficient of the two-way interaction will be significant and positive because the attributes are complements. If the coefficient is negative and significant, the attributes are substitutes, which invalidates the multiplying model.

Each statistical test has an associated graphical test. It is unwise to conduct the statistical tests without graphing the corresponding data because replicated designs have considerable statistical power that increases with the number of replications. Thus not infrequently one obtains a precise (statistically significant) estimate of an effect that is virtually zero. Graphs provide visual evidence of the form of a consumer's decision process that is complemented by statistical tests and, hence, offer insights into process that cannot be obtained from consideration of statistical results alone. Thus by graphing the data before conducting statistical tests, one should be able to anticipate the test results.

Figure 2.1 provides hypothetical examples of (a) additive, (b) multiplicative or complementary, and (c) substitutive decision processes. Figure 2.1(a) demonstrates that additive processes manifest themselves as a series of parallel curves, indicating that the effects of S_{1p} on the ratings are independent of the effects of S_{2q}. In contrast, Figure (2.1b) indicates that in the multiplicative case, curves of data corresponding to levels of S_{1p} diverge (grow further apart) as a function of the levels of S_{2q}. Thus, as the levels of both S_{1p} and S_{2q} become more attractive, a subject's responses should become more extreme. Figure 2.1(c) shows that if attributes are substitutes, attractive levels of S_{1p} are relatively unaffected by unattractive levels of S_{2q} versa. Hence a subject finds the best levels of the two attributes almost equally attractive, and having both attractive levels is only slightly more attractive than having either alone.

2.1.3 THREE-ATTRIBUTE (FACTOR) DESIGNS

The concepts and method of approach for two-attribute problems generalize to three-attribute problems, with some minor additional complications. Let us therefore consider the breakdown in the variation in R_{pqr}:

Variation in R_{pqr} = Variation due to $V(S_{1p})$
+ Variation due to $V(S_{2q})$
+ Variation due to $V(S_{3r})$

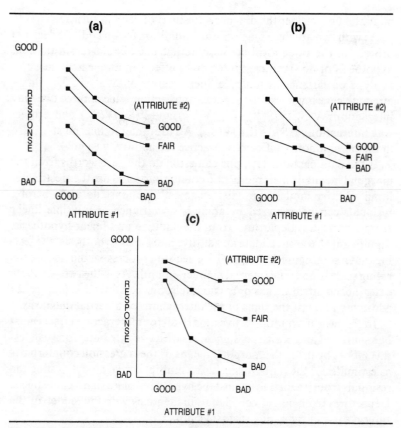

Figure 2.1 Graphical Forms of Additive, Complementary, and Substitutive Decision Processes

+ Variation due to $V(S_{1p})$ & $V(S_{2q})$
+ Variation due to $V(S_{1p})$ & $V(S_{3r})$
+ Variation due to $V(S_{2q})$ & $V(S_{3r})$
+ Variation due to $V(S_{1p})$ & $V(S_{2q})$ & $V(S_{3r})$.

As previously discussed, with a single replication one cannot test the significance of the variance components. Moreover, without three levels for each attribute, one cannot fully diagnose or test the various conjoint models discussed in Chapter 1: (a) additive, (b) multiplicative, (c) distributive, (d) dual-distributive, or (e) multilinear. Bearing that caveat in mind, let us consider the diagnosis (testing) of each in turn.

As with two attributes, a necessary condition for an additive decision process in the three-attribute case is that one should retain the null hypothesis of no significant interaction effects in a repeated measures analysis of variance or multiple linear regression analysis. The three-attribute case involves four separate interaction effects: three two-way interactions, $V(S_{1p})V(S_{2q})$, $V(S_{1p})V(S_{3r})$, and $V(S_{2q})V(S_{3r})$, and a three-way interaction, $V(S_{1p})V(S_{2q})V(S_{3r})$. All four interactions must be zero in theory and nonsignificant in practice for additivity to hold.

If the data pass this test, one can estimate the part-worths from the marginal means or their regression counterparts and use these estimates in an additive model to predict a subject's response data. As before, residuals can be analyzed by analysis of variance or multiple linear regression to test departures from the additive and linear hypothesis. Significant effects invalidate an additive and linear hypothesis, suggesting that a subject used a nonadditive decision process, or did not use the rating scale in an equal interval manner, or both. As in the two-attribute case, if each attribute has only two levels, one can only accept or reject additivity and test the signs of the interactions as a partial diagnosis.

In the case of a multiplicative model, all four interaction effects must be significant and positively signed. As with two attributes, one can test this model by using the marginal means or the regression counterparts as estimates of the part-worths in the multiplicative model, testing the residuals from prediction against the hypothesis of no significant effects. Departures from null effects signals inadequacy with the model, or the subject's use of the rating scale, or both.

A distributive model is implied if only two of the two-way interactions and all of the main effects are significant. If other interactions are significant, the distributive model is rejected. Also, the sign of the two interactions must be positive, implying a complementary relationship. Hence, if either sign is negative, the distributive hypothesis must be rejected in favor of either a substitution model (if both signs are negative), or a multilinear model (if one is negative and one is positive). Whichever result is obtained, one can estimate the marginal means or the corresponding regression parameters, using these estimates in the model of interest to predict a subject's response data. As before, residuals from prediction can be tested using analysis of variance or multiple linear regression models to support or disconfirm a particular conjoint model of interest.

In the case of the dual-distributive model, only one two-way interaction effect can be significant, and the sign of this effect must be positive. A negative sign disconfirms a dual-distributive hypothesis in favor of a model with one independent (additive) attribute and two attribute substitutes (a multilinear model). Whatever model is indicated, one can estimate the part-worths from the marginal means or their regression counterparts and use these estimates to predict a subject's data, testing the residuals in an analysis of variance or multiple linear regression analysis. Any departure from the null model disconfirms the particular model of interest, or warns that the subject may not have used the rating scale in an equal interval manner, or both.

As in the two-attribute case, effects should be graphically analyzed. The three-attribute case requires one to graph the three main effects, the three two-way interactions, and the single three-way interaction. All graphs complement the associated statistical tests for the same reasons given in the two-attribute case. One should anticipate the statistical results from the graphs.

2.1.4 M-ATTRIBUTE (FACTOR) DESIGNS

We hope it is clear that the concepts and method of approach already discussed with reference to two- and three-attribute designs, extend to M-attribute designs. As one increases the number of attributes, the number of main effects increases linearly, but the number of interactions increases exponentially. So, with four attributes, there are four main effects, six two-way interactions, four three-way interactions, and one four-way interaction. All effects must be tested to diagnose an appropriate conjoint model for a subject. Furthermore, attributes have to have more than two levels to adequately test each model of interest statistically.

Obviously, therefore, the practical difficulties of conducting experiments to diagnose and test conjoint models for single subjects greatly increase once one considers more than three attributes, or more than two levels per attribute. Hence most practical conjoint studies involving four or more attributes at two or more levels rely on some type of fractional factorial design and/or a single replication per subject.

2.2 Fractional Factorial Designs

A fractional factorial experiment is a sample of treatments selected from a complete factorial design. One must be cautious of fractional designs because, without all possible combinations of attribute levels (complete factorials), information is lost. Not only is information lost in that tests of some (often a large number) effects cannot be conducted, but information lost is confounded with information obtained. *Confounded* means that some effects are correlated (often perfectly or highly correlated) with other effects. That is, effects that can be estimated are linear combinations of effects that cannot be estimated (often "perfect" linear combinations). Such correlations among observed and/or unobserved effects are termed "collinearities" in econometrics and statistics.

An amusing way to think about collinearities in fractions is to consider the following riddle, familiar to many from childhood: How many legs does a sheep have if we call a tail a leg? Some answer four, and others five. The correct answer is four, because calling a tail a leg doesn't make it a leg. Fractional factorial designs are like the riddle: One calls a particular effect a leg, but because one calls it a leg doesn't make it a leg. Let us examine a fractional design in detail to learn why calling an effect an effect doesn't make it one.

Figure 2.2 displays both the complete factorial and two one-half fractions of a $2 \times 2 \times 2$ (or usually, 2^3) design. Levels of the three two-level attributes are represented as -1 and $+1$, respectively. We use -1 and $+1$ rather than, say 1 and 2, because -1 and $+1$ are orthogonal polynomial codes (see Sections 2.2.1 and 3.2.1.6) for two-level factors, and they can be used to define the interactions by simple multiplication of the codes in the columns that represent each attribute. Thus the two-and three-way interactions can be (and were) generated by multiplying the codes in the columns representing each main effect to obtain the corresponding two-and three-way cross-product columns (interactions).

Figure 2.2 reveals that both one-half fractions contain columns that are duplicates of one another. In particular, S_1 is exactly negatively correlated with $S_2 \times S_3$ in Fraction A, and exactly positively correlated in Fraction B. Thus S_1 is perfectly confounded with the $S_2 \times S_3$ interaction, and the effect of S_1 can be estimated only if $S_2 \times S_3$ is equal to zero. Otherwise, the effect represented by the column S_1 contains BOTH the effects of S_1 and $S_2 \times S_3$, and these effects cannot be separated. Similarly, S_2 is perfectly correlated with $S_1 \times S_3$, and S_3 is perfectly correlated with $S_1 \times S_2$. Like S_1, neither the S_2 nor the S_3 estimates can be interpreted unless both $S_1 \times S_2$ and $S_1 \times S_3$ are exactly zero. Finally, the three-way interactions column labeled $S_1 S_2 S_3$ is perfectly correlated with the intercept or grand mean. Thus every interaction column in Fractions A and B is perfectly confounded with some other effect of potential interest. Hence we can call the column labeled S_1, "S_1," but it is

| Main Effects | | | Two-Way Interactions | | | Three-Way Interactions |
S_1	S_2	2_3	$S_1 S_2$	$S_1 S_3$	$S_2 S_3$	$S_1 S_2 S_3$
−1	−1	−1	+1	+1	+1	−1
−1	−1	+1	+1	−1	−1	+1
−1	+1	−1	−1	+1	−1	+1
−1	+1	+1	−1	−1	+1	−1
+1	−1	−1	−1	−1	+1	+1
+1	−1	+1	−1	+1	−1	−1
+1	+1	−1	+1	−1	−1	−1
+1	+1	+1	+1	+1	+1	+1

Fraction A

−1	−1	+1	+1	−1	−1	+1
−1	+1	−1	−1	+1	+1	+1
+1	−1	−1	−1	−1	−1	+1
+1	+1	+1	+1	+1	+1	+1

Fraction B

−1	−1	−1	+1	+1	+1	−1
−1	+1	+1	−1	−1	+1	−1
+1	−1	+1	−1	+1	−1	−1
+1	+1	−1	+1	−1	−1	−1

Figure 2.2: The 2^3 Design and the Two One-Half Fractions That Can Be Generated from It

S_1 only if $S_2 \times S_3$ equals zero. Calling a tail a leg doesn't make it a leg either for a sheep or for a column of a fractional design.

Admittedly, one would rarely use the fractions in Figure 2.2 because consumers can almost always evaluate at least eight attribute combinations. However, sometimes attribute levels consist of long verbal descriptions, pictures, models, or in general, somewhat complex information, and one might feel (or find in pilot work) that asking respondents to evaluate more than four treatments would be too complicated, difficult, time consuming, or otherwise burdensome. In such cases, one might wish as few treatments as possible.

Let us, however, consider a more realistic problem involving a one-half fraction of a 2^4. The 15 possible effects of four two-level attributes are displayed in Figure 2.3, which makes it easy to see the confoundment structure of this particular fractional design. First, note that columns labeled S_1, S_2 and S_3 contain the complete 2^3; hence the column labeled S_4 must be a leg. In fact, the S_4 column is perfectly correlated with the column labeled $S_1 \times S_2 \times S_3$. Thus the effect represented by the column labeled S_4 is either S_4, $S_1 \times S_2 \times S_3$ or some combination of both, and unless $S_1 \times S_2 \times S_3$ is zero, these effects are confounded.

Similarly, S_1 is confounded with $S_2 \times S_3 \times S_4$, S_2 is confounded with $S_1 \times S_3 \times S_4$ and S_3 is confounded with $S_1 \times S_2 \times S_4$. Importantly, none of the main effects is confounded with two-way interactions, but each of the two-way interactions is confounded with one other two-way interaction. Thus we would say that this design permits estimates of main effects unconfounded by significant two-way interactions but not unconfounded by unobserved, significant three-way interactions. Furthermore, although some two-way interactions can be estimated, they are confounded with other two-way interactions. To use this design one must assume that all three-way interactions are negligible and half of the two-way interactions are equal to zero (one must decide which ones are equal to zero). The four-way interaction is confounded with the intercept or grand mean, and thus one must also assume this interaction to be negligible.

The design in Figure 2.3 is typical of fractional factorial designs. To use fractions one must assume that the unobserved effects that are confounded with the effects of interest are equal to zero. If such assumptions are untenable or if one is uncertain about their satisfaction in a particular design being considered, one should consider alternative designs with different confoundment properties. In that vein, the following considerations can be used as a guide to choosing fractional designs (see, Green, 1974):

(1) Can it be assumed that all interaction effects are equal to zero; that is, is an additive model appropriate? If the answer is yes, select any main effects plan that suits one's purposes. A main effects plan is a fractional factorial design that permits one to estimate only the main effects, assuming negligible interactions. If the answer is no, proceed to consideration 2.

(2) Can it be assumed that only selected interaction effects are significant in addition to main effects? That is, is some form of a multilinear model appropriate? If the answer is yes, select a design plan that permits one to estimate all main effects plus the selected interaction effects of interest. Such plans are often called "main effects plus selected interactions" plans. If the answer is no, proceed to consideration 3.

(3) Can it be assumed that only two-way interactions are significant, but which ones are significant is not known (or perhaps all are significant)? That is, is some form of a multilinear model appropriate? If the

| Main Effects | | | | Two-, Three-, and Four-Way Interactions | | | | | | | | | | |
S_1	S_2	S_3	S_4	$S_1 S_2$	$S_1 S_3$	$S_1 S_4$	$S_2 S_3$	$S_2 S_4$	$S_3 S_4$	$S_1 S_2 S_3$	$S_1 S_2 S_4$	$S_1 S_3 S_4$	$S_2 S_3 S_4$	$S_1 S_2 S_3 S_4$
-1	-1	-1	-1	+1	+1	+1	+1	+1	+1	-1	-1	-1	-1	+1
-1	-1	+1	+1	+1	-1	-1	-1	-1	+1	+1	+1	-1	-1	+1
-1	+1	-1	+1	-1	+1	-1	-1	+1	-1	+1	-1	+1	-1	+1
-1	+1	+1	-1	-1	-1	+1	+1	-1	-1	-1	+1	+1	-1	+1
+1	-1	-1	+1	-1	-1	+1	+1	-1	-1	+1	-1	-1	+1	+1
+1	-1	+1	-1	-1	+1	-1	-1	+1	-1	-1	+1	-1	+1	+1
+1	+1	-1	-1	+1	-1	-1	-1	-1	+1	-1	-1	+1	+1	+1
+1	+1	+1	+1	+1	+1	+1	+1	+1	+1	+1	+1	+1	+1	+1

Figure 2.3: A One-Half Fraction of the 2^4 Design

answer is yes, select a fractional design that permits independent estimation of all main effects and two-way interactions, assuming negligible higher-order interactions. If the answer is no, proceed to consideration 4.

(4) Can it be assumed that no interactions higher than three-way are significant? That is, is some form of a multilinear model appropriate? If the answer is yes, choose a design that permits one to estimate all main and two-way interaction effects independent of significant, but unobserved three-way interactions. If three-way interactions are actually of interest, choose a design that permits one to estimate all main effects, two-way, and three-way interactions independently of one another, but not independently of unobserved but assumed nonsignificant higher-order interactions.

(5) Virtually no one (probably exactly no one) tries to estimate interactions of an order higher than three in practical applications. That is not to say that such interactions are not significant or meaningful; rather, it is only to say that except for small problems, this is a Herculean task. Moreover, except in special cases, it is usually unclear how to interpret such interactions.

The logic of the above design considerations rests on the well-known fact that in almost all cases involving real data, the following generalizations hold about significant effects: (a) Main effects explain the largest amount of variance in response data, often 80% or more; (b) two-way interactions account for the next largest proportion of variance, although this rarely exceeds 3%-6%; (c) three-way interactions account for even smaller proportions of variance, rarely more than 2%-3% (usually 0.5%-1%); and (d) higher-order terms account for minuscule proportions of variance.

The general strategy in choosing a fractional design is to protect against sources of variation that are not estimated, are confounded with what is estimated, and are likely to produce the most bias in parameters that are estimated. It normally suffices to protect main effects and two-way interactions against possibly significant three-way interactions (three-way interactions rarely are of interest). Hence the basic decision in choosing a fractional factorial design for a particular problem is which interaction columns to confound with which effects: One normally tries to confound the effects of most interest with effects that are unlikely to be significant or, if they are significant, are unlikely to cause much bias in the parameters that are estimated.

Thus one tries to confound main effects and two-way interactions with the highest order interactions possible. In the design illustrated in

Figure 2.3, main effects are confounded with three-way interactions, which are the highest order effects aside from the single four-way interaction; and the two-way interactions are confounded with each other. The 2^4 design is somewhat small; so it would be difficult to improve on this confoundment structure without more than eight attribute combinations.

Figure 2.4 illustrates a one-half fraction of the 2^5 design involving 16 attribute combinations. In this design all main and two-way interaction effects in this design are confounded with higher-order effects; both main effects and two-way interactions can be estimated independently of one another but not independently of unobserved higher-order interactions.

The designs illustrated in Figures 2.3 and 2.4 suggest that one can create designs with the statistical properties one wants by using orthogonal polynomial codes to represent attribute levels, creating all two- and three-way interaction cross-products, and checking the resulting confoundment structure using principal components analysis. One cannot understand the confoundment structure of a design by visually checking the correlation matrix because an effect may be a linear combination of more than just one other effect. One therefore should be cautious about computerized design generators that ask one to visually inspect a correlation matrix representing the effects in a design to see if the correlations are "satisfactory."

In fact, if one is unfamiliar with design concepts and properties of fractional designs, one might wish to experiment with various confoundment alternatives and examine the resulting design properties. One must understand the exact properties of a fractional design in order to decide whether these properties are acceptable. For example, many applied conjoint studies use main effects "plans" in which main effects are confounded with two-way interactions. This is almost always a bad idea because one generally cannot assume that such interactions are negligible; and if they are not negligible, the estimates of main effects will be biased. Because such bias can be considerable, it makes sense to take the time to understand the statistical properties of design alternatives. At the least, managers should insist that their conjoint studies are based on appropriate designs to minimize the possibility of biased results.

Practical fractional factorial designs can be found in a number of published design catalogs containing listings of various designs and their statistical properties. To use such catalogs, one states the design

S_1	S_2	S_3	S_4	S_5	S_1S_2	S_1S_3	S_1S_4	S_1S_5	S_2S_3	S_2S_4	S_2S_5	S_3S_4	S_3S_5	S_4S_5
−1	−1	−1	−1	−1	+1	+1	+1	+1	+1	+1	+1	+1	+1	+1
−1	−1	−1	+1	+1	+1	+1	−1	−1	+1	−1	−1	−1	−1	+1
−1	−1	+1	−1	+1	+1	−1	+1	−1	−1	+1	−1	−1	+1	−1
−1	−1	+1	+1	−1	+1	−1	−1	+1	−1	−1	+1	+1	−1	−1
−1	+1	−1	−1	+1	−1	+1	+1	−1	−1	−1	+1	+1	−1	−1
−1	+1	−1	+1	−1	−1	+1	−1	+1	−1	+1	−1	−1	+1	−1
−1	+1	+1	−1	−1	−1	−1	+1	+1	+1	−1	−1	−1	−1	+1
−1	+1	+1	+1	+1	−1	−1	−1	−1	+1	+1	+1	+1	+1	+1
+1	−1	−1	−1	+1	−1	−1	−1	+1	+1	+1	−1	+1	−1	−1
+1	−1	−1	+1	−1	−1	−1	+1	−1	+1	−1	+1	−1	+1	−1
+1	−1	+1	−1	−1	−1	+1	−1	−1	−1	+1	+1	−1	−1	+1
+1	−1	+1	+1	+1	−1	+1	+1	+1	−1	−1	−1	+1	+1	+1
+1	+1	−1	−1	−1	+1	−1	−1	−1	−1	−1	−1	+1	+1	+1
+1	+1	−1	+1	+1	+1	−1	+1	+1	−1	+1	+1	−1	−1	+1
+1	+1	+1	−1	+1	+1	+1	−1	+1	+1	−1	+1	−1	+1	−1
+1	+1	+1	+1	−1	+1	+1	+1	−1	+1	+1	−1	+1	−1	−1

Figure 2.4: A One-Half Fraction of the 2^5 Factorial Design

requirements for a particular problem as per Considerations 1 to 4 above and selects a design with the necessary properties. Some useful design catalogs include Hahn and Shapiro (1966), Conner and Zelen (1959), and McLean and Anderson (1984).

2.2.1 USING ORTHOGONAL POLYNOMIAL CODES TO DETERMINE THE PROPERTIES OF PARTICULAR FRACTIONAL DESIGNS

A word of caution about computerized design generators and/or design catalogs is in order: Some designs in these sources are created using a geometric definition of the main and interaction effects. Designs generated by a geometric definition should be used only with analysis of variance models and are useful if one wants to make a global test of a certain effect, but is not interested in the algebraic shape or form of the effect. In contrast, product definitions of designs permit one to test for various polynomial forms such as X and X^2 that have algebraic interpretations. One can determine if a design satisfies the product rule by using orthogonal polynomial codes to represent the main effects, creating all the interaction effects as cross-products of these codes (see also Section 3.2.1.6). A principal components analysis of the correlation matrix of the main and interaction effects defined by the product rule reveals whether the design satisfies the product definition: The polynomial effects to be estimated must be independent of one another. All complete factorials but not all fractional factorials satisfy the product definition; in general, if all two-way interactions can be estimated, a design should satisfy the product definition.

Figures 2.2 and 2.3 illustrate the product definition of the interaction effects as the products of the orthogonal polynomial codes for two-level attributes (−1, +1). Figure 2.5 illustrates the use of orthogonal polynomial codes for three-level attributes to satisfy the product definition of main effects and two-way interactions for a 3×4 design. Unless one uses qualitative attributes with more than three levels, linear and quadratic main and interaction effects ordinarily will suffice to describe a consumer's response surface. Linear and quadratic codes provide exact estimates of the part-worth utility parameters for three-level quantitative attributes; and one rarely needs additional polynomial codes to describe the effects of quantitative attributes with more than three levels. Tables of orthogonal codes for use with qualitative attributes or with quantitative attributes whose numerical levels are evenly spaced can be found in many statistics texts (e.g., Hays, 1973, or Figure 3.3).

A (4)			B (3)		AL	AL	AQ	AQ	AC	AC
LN	QD	CU	LN	QD	BL	BQ	BL	BQ	BL	BQ
−3	+1	−1	−1	+1	+3	−3	−1	+1	+1	−1
−3	+1	−1	0	−2	0	+6	0	−2	0	+2
−3	+1	−1	+1	+1	−3	−3	+1	+1	−1	−1
−1	−1	+3	−1	+1	+1	−1	+1	−1	−3	+3
−1	−1	+3	0	−2	0	+2	0	+2	0	−6
−1	−1	+3	+1	+1	−1	−1	−1	−1	+3	+3
+1	−1	−3	−1	+1	−1	+1	+1	−1	+3	−3
+1	−1	−3	0	−2	0	−2	0	+2	0	+6
+1	−1	−3	+1	+1	+1	+1	−1	−1	−3	−3
+3	+1	+1	−1	+1	−3	+3	−1	+1	−1	+1
+3	+1	+1	0	−2	0	−6	0	−2	0	−2
+3	+1	+1	+1	+1	+3	+1	+1	+1	+1	+1

NOTE: LN = Linear; QD = Quadratic; CU = Cubic.

Figure 2.5: The Production Definition of the 4 × 3 Design Using Orthogonal Polynomial Codes to Define the Effects

Robson (1959) offers a method for constructing orthogonal polynomials if the levels of quantitative attributes are unevenly spaced.

2.3 Analysis of Data from Factorial Conjoint Experiments

In this section we assume that one has determined an appropriate functional form for a conjoint model using the graphical and statistical tests outlined in Section 2.1. The object of this section is to explain how to develop a parsimonious representation of the rating data consistent with a particular conjoint model form. We also assume that one is interested in interpolating to unobserved treatment combinations, and multiple linear regression models can be versatile tools for developing such approximations.

Consider the marginal mean of Attribute S_{1p}. This marginal mean is a function of the corresponding levels of the attribute itself as varied in the experiment. That is,

$$R_{p..} = g(S_{1p}) + e_{p..}, \qquad [2.4]$$

where all terms have been defined previously, except g, a mapping.

If S_{1p} is a numerical or quantitative variable such as price, we can write the mapping g as follows with no loss of generality:

$$R_{p..} = a_0 + a_1 S_{1p} + a_2 S_{1p}^2 + e_{p..}, \qquad [2.5]$$

where all terms have been defined earlier, except the a's, which are regression constants. If S_{1p} has only three levels ($p = 1, 2, 3$), then equation 2.5 exactly defines the marginal means. This result follows from a well-known theorem in elementary calculus: If there are P points on a graph, a curve represented by a polynomial of degree P-1 will pass exactly through each of the P points.

The connection between analysis of variance and multiple linear regression also can be seen in this result: A multiple regression model in multiple polynomial form and an analysis of variance model produce identical statistical results because the analysis of variance partitions the variance in the response variable into independent pieces, each of which is defined by deviations about various means that define the effects of interest. The multiple linear regression model in polynomial form also partitions each effect into independent sources of variation through the use of polynomial or dummy-coded terms.

A multiple polynomial regression model will exactly fit the means that define the effects in an analysis of variance; hence the variance accounted for by the independent partitions is the same for each model. Regression models are useful because they can partition the variance into meaningful polynomial pieces that permit inferences to be made about functional form. It is this use of multiple regression models that is of practical interest in approximating consumer decision processes.

Suppose, for example, one has designed and executed a 2^3 factorial experiment and has obtained two replications from each subject (see, e.g., Figure 1.2). The following regression model(s) define the response data:

$$R_{1pqr} = a_0 + a_1 S_{1p} + a_2 S_{2q} + a_3 S_{3r} + a_4 S_{1p} S_{2q} + a_5 S_{1p} S_{3r} \qquad [2.5a]$$
$$+ a_6 S_{2q} S_{3r} + a_7 S_{1p} S_{2q} S_{3r},$$

and

$$R_{2pqr} = b_0 + b_1 S_{1p} + b_2 S_{2q} + b_3 S_{3r} + b_4 S_{1p} S_{2q} + b_5 S_{1p} S_{3r} \qquad [2.5b]$$
$$+ b_6 S_{2q} S_{3r} + b_7 S_{1p} S_{2q} S_{3r},$$

where all terms have been defined before, except the a's and the b's, which are regression parameters estimated from, respectively, the first and second replications. No error term is specified in either model because no degrees of freedom remain for error in either replication. The eight observations in each replication are subject to the same theorem that applies to P points on a graph because the eight degrees of freedom in each replication can be captured by a polynomial of degree seven.

From this experiment one can estimate 6 marginal means (two for each attribute because each level of each attribute corresponds to a marginal mean); 12 two-way interaction means (four for each pair of attributes: the means for the joint occurrence of Level 1 of Attribute 1 and Level 1 of Attribute 2; Level 1 of Attribute 1 and Level 2 of Attribute 2, and so on); and 8 three-way interaction means (one for each joint triple occurrence of attribute levels: 111, 112, 121, and so on). Each marginal mean can be defined by a regression equation that is linear in the corresponding attribute levels because each attribute has two levels: Two marginal means constitute two points on a graph; hence only linear relationships can define the main effect of each attribute. The inter-actions of two-level attributes can be represented by vectors with two levels (-1, +1; see Figures 2.2-2.4); hence each two-way interaction has one degree of freedom, despite the four means that can be estimated. The four means are accounted for by the two main effects and the single two-way interaction column—a polynomial of degree three to describe four points.

Diagnosis of an appropriate conjoint model specification proceeds as follows for the replicated 2^3 experiment described above (our diagnosis, however, will be incomplete because each attribute has only two levels): Calculate the mean parameter for each effect from both regression equations. The mean parameter for the main effect of S_1 is $(a_1 + b_1)/2$, and the mean parameter for the interaction of S_1 and S_2 is $(a_4 + b_4)/2$. All other effects can be defined similarly. The standard error for the main effect of S_1 is estimated by dividing the standard deviation of the empirical distribution of the two regression parameters representing S_1 by the square root of the number of parameter estimates. The statistic defined by dividing the mean parameter by its estimated standard error is distributed as a t distribution, and can be tested in the usual way. Each test has one degree of freedom in this example.

If each attribute had three levels instead of two, both regression models represented by equations 2.5a and 2.5b would have contained 26 terms plus an intercept. Each of the three main effects has two degrees of freedom, each two-way interaction has four degrees of freedom, and the three-way interaction has eight degrees of freedom (6 + 12 + 8 + the intercept). The analysis is identical to the two-level case above, except that 26 effects would need to be tested instead of 7. Hence the testing procedure is the same regardless of how large the design is or how many effects are estimated. If one uses a fractional design, the analysis is conducted in the same way, except that only the estimable effects are included in the regression model(s). If subjects complete only one replication, one can estimate the parameters of interest; but statistical tests of the parameters based on mean square error (residual mean square) should be regarded with considerable suspicion. We will deal with practical methods for handling this problem in Chapter 3.

2.4 Analysis of Individual Differences

Often in conjoint studies, one wishes to account for individual differences in the parameters of utility functions and to identify groups (market segments) of relatively homogeneous individuals with similar utility functions. Thus the question of accounting for individual differences arises. There are several ways to analyze individual differences in conjoint response data, but we will restrict our discussion to two general methods: (a) statistical analysis of covariates and (b) cluster analysis.

2.4.1 COVARIANCE ANALYSIS OF INDIVIDUAL DIFFERENCES

If individuals respond to all treatments of a particular fraction of a factorial design, regression models can be used to approximate their responses to the design variables. The estimated regression parameters can be treated as dependent variables in a second analysis in which various measures of individual differences (covariates) are explanatory variables. Such variables can be market segmentation measures often observed in practical research problems, such as age, sex, income, education, and family size; or measures of product usage, media usage, and distribution outlet usage; or so-called psychographic measures that define consumer life-styles, interests, opinions, and values. Such variables are called covariates because they are not controlled or manipulated in the experiment but "covary" with the responses.

A useful statistical approach to this problem is Multiple ANalysis Of VAriance. MANOVA is the multiple dependent variable analog of analysis of variance. To apply MANOVA to the analysis of individual differences in utility functions, one treats the individuals' regression coefficient vectors as dependent variables and the matrix of individual-difference measures (segmentation covariates) as independent variables. In a MANOVA analysis a multiple linear regression analysis is performed on each vector of regression coefficients using the covariates as predictor variables; and an analysis of linear combinations of the regression parameters is conducted in which the covariates are explanatory variables (see Section 3.3.10 for an example).

Hence MANOVA provides two different types of statistical information: (a) relationships between each vector of regression coefficients and the covariates (for example, does the effect of price decrease as income increases?) and (b) relationships among linear combinations of the coefficient vectors and segmentation measures (vectors of conjoint regression coefficients usually are correlated across samples of subjects: For example, subjects who have a high utility for whitener in toothpaste may also have high utility for breath freshener).

Canonical correlation analysis can also be used to identify linear combinations of conjoint coefficients and segmentation variables. The component or factor scores derived from decomposing the correlations among the regression coefficient vectors can be analyzed as a function of the component or factor scores vectors derived from decomposing the correlations among the segmentation measures. A disadvantage of this approach is that one must subjectively interpret the empirical content of the score vectors derived from decomposing the two correlation matrices. Recently, Haggerty (1987) demonstrated that a principal components analysis of a subject $\times$ subject correlation matrix of the ratings response vectors (a so-called Q-analysis) produces optimal segments in terms of the fits of linear-in-the-parameters-and-additive conjoint models to the component score vectors.

2.4.2 CLUSTERING SIMILAR SUBJECTS

K-Means Cluster analysis can be applied to subjects' vectors of category ratings or estimated conjoint part-worth (regression) parameters to derive "benefit segments" (e.g., Urban and Hauser, 1980: 259-266). In this approach, one uses cluster analysis to group subjects according to some measure of distance, relatedness, or similarity between their vectors of ratings data or regression coefficients. Once clusters or "segments" are identified, one normally tests whether the segments differ significantly on various segmentation measures of interest. Multinomial logit discriminant analysis (see Chapter 4) can be used to test for between-segment differences. Unlike conventional discriminant analysis, one does not have to assume that the explanatory segmentation measures variables are multinormal, continuous variables, one need only assume that they can be categorized. An additional advantage is that the estimated discriminant parameters can be interpreted like regression parameters in terms of their effect on the probability of cluster membership.

Alternatively, one might subject the cluster membership measures to a CHAID analysis (Perreault and Barksdale, 1980). CHAID is a regressionlike procedure for the analysis of interaction effects in nominal data. The dependent cluster membership measure can be decomposed into a series of independent associations with categorical segmentation measures according to a chi-square criterion. The result is a series of statistically significant, treelike links between various segmentation measure categories and each segment.

In the next chapter on practical problem solving, we shall return to many of the issues and techniques discussed in this chapter, illustrating their application to practical problems.

3. PRACTICAL APPLICATIONS OF CONJOINT THEORY AND METHODS

3.0 Introduction

This chapter describes a variety of ways to apply the theory and methods discussed in the first two chapters to practical problems. Several steps are required to develop conjoint approximations to consumer judgment and decision processes that can forecast what consumers are likely to do in response to various actions or policies of interest:

(1) One must understand the decision problem and environment faced by the target individuals of interest, including an identification of the key determinant decision attributes;
(2) One must develop a product-positioning data base in which each target individual associates brands (alternatives) with particular levels of the determinant decision attributes (it may not be possible to do this in all problem situations);
(3) One must design a conjoint experiment to understand how the target individuals integrate the decision attributes, that is, how the target individuals evaluate multiattribute alternatives or brands;
(4) One must identify measurable and actionable market segments that are likely to respond differently to different management policy actions; and

(5) One must create a choice simulation system to forecast how the target individuals are likely to choose among different brands or multiattribute alternatives offered in the marketplace.

In addition to these steps, a major consideration in any conjoint study is the identification of and sample selection from the target population of interest. Let us discuss each of the major steps in turn.

3.1 Understanding the Decision Problem

Exploratory research can provide important insights into a research problem by identifying pitfalls and exceptions to generalizations and abstractions that researchers may make about consumer decision making. For example, great care must be taken to ensure that all (or at least as many as possible) of the determinant decision attributes are identified and expressed in terms understood by the individuals to be studied. Some attributes require visual representation, some require elaborate verbal and visual descriptions, and others require actual products, prototypes or scale models to ensure that the information will be understood. In short, one must develop a preconceived model of how consumers make decisions in a particular situation. The conceptual theory outlined in Chapter 1 provides a general framework for such a mental model, but one must develop a specific framework for each research problem of interest.

Exploratory research into consumer decision making is usually qualitative in nature, often involving focused group discussions, semistructured telephone interviews, or depth interviews. Use of structured mail or telephone surveys is rare, except as a test of hypotheses based on qualitative research results. Information about design, conduct, and analysis of exploratory research projects can be found in Lehmann (1985), Churchill (1983), or Kinnear and Taylor (1983). Miller (1983) summarizes related literature in sociology.

3.2 Identifying Determinant Attributes

There is no present consensus as to the "best" approach to attribute identification. Kelly's (1955) personal construct theory has been useful in past research (see, e.g., Levin et al., 1983; Green and Tull, 1978: 561-562). Kelly's approach involves asking individuals to compare existing products or services three at a time, indicating in what ways they are similar and different. "Constructs" are derived from a content analysis of individuals' responses. In some applications the constructs are rated by the individual(s) and then subjected to a factor analysis.

Our applied work often has relied on one or more unstructured (except for topic) focused group interviews, combined with a series of semistructured, open-ended questions, such as the following:

(1) Which products (services) in this product class do you buy (own), or would you consider buying (owning)?
(2) Which products (services) in this product class do you not buy (own), or would you consider not buying (owning)?
(3) You said that you would buy (own) or would consider buying (owning) brand(s) (products in Question 1 are now repeated). What is it about these products that makes them attractive to you?
(4) You said that you do not buy (own) brand(s) (products in Question 2 are repeated) or would not consider buying (owning) them. What is it about these products that is unattractive to you?
(5) Thinking about the products (services) that you buy (own) or would consider buying (owning), what would the producers or sellers of these products (services) have to do to them to influence you not to buy (own) them?
(6) Thinking about the products (services) that you said you do not buy (own) or would not consider buying (owning), what would the producers or sellers of these products (services) have to do to them to influence you to buy (own) them?

Normally, two or more trained analysts independently study the answers to the foregoing questions, analyze them for meaning and content, and classify them into mutually exclusive and exhaustive categories. The categories are reconciled into a single classification, and the number of times (frequency) that each category is mentioned is tabulated. Each question produces a different frequency distribution for each construct category; the frequencies are cross-tabulated and compared.

The redundancy encourages subjects to look at both positive and negative aspects of the antecedents of a decision. If one wants to be expedient, however, Questions 1-4 usually suffice to develop a fairly comprehensive list of possible decision attributes. Tabulating the frequency with which subjects' responses to Questions 1-4 are associated with each construct category permits one to make (arbitrary) decisions about which constructs (decision attributes) to use in a conjoint study. For example, we often use the (arbitrary) criterion that a construct must be mentioned by at least 5% of the respondents to be used in a study.

Once a list of attributes is determined, two other considerations arise:

(1) Are the decision attributes actionable? Respondents often use composite or "fuzzy" concepts to convey their reasons for purchasing behavior, such as "quality" or "convenience." Such concepts may mean different things to different people, and they are insufficiently specific to inform managers about the consequences of taking actions to change their brand's position on the concepts. Thus vague attribute concepts often need further definition, and follow-up research may be needed to further define the constructs. Conjoint techniques can be used to define fuzzy constructs such as quality and convenience. For example, combinations of actionable, measurable variables can be designed to define particular fuzzy constructs; and category-response scales can be used to measure these constructs. In this way, attributes such as convenience or quality can be defined to be a function of specific actionable or measurable variables by observing how individuals rate the degree of convenience or the amount of quality produced by combinations of actionable, measurable variables.

(2) The language and terms or the way in which an attribute's variation is to be communicated to respondents must be developed. Ordinarily, if attributes can be expressed verbally, appropriate ways to communicate the concept information can be inferred from transcripts of focused group discussions or replies to semistructured interview questions. Otherwise, research must be conducted into appropriate vehicles for communicating the decision attributes. Every research project is unique in this respect, so it is difficult to generalize; however, it is very important to ensure that attribute information is properly communicated to the target individuals. Myers and Shocker (1981) develop a general typology of attributes and discuss their use in conjoint and other types of research.

3.3 Developing Product Positioning Measures

The previous section discussed ways to identify determinant attributes, but not how to decide upon their levels. This decision normally is less complicated than identifying attributes because the range of the attributes often is known and fixed by technological, market, or other constraints. In some cases, however, one must use management judgment, interviews with experts, or previous experience to develop ranges of levels that satisfy research objectives and are meaningful to subjects.

Several makes and models of automobiles are listed below. You may not be familiar with all of them, but if you have opinions based on what you've read, seen, or heard, we would like to know them. Circle the letter that you feel best describes your opinion about each automobile's selling price, miles per gallon, warranty period, and ride comfort. If you know nothing about a particular automobile, please circle the category labeled "I don't know."

		Mazda 626	Toyota Corolla	Nissan 200 SX
Selling (sticker) price				
a.	$7,500	a	a	a
b.	$8,250	b	b	b
.		.	.	.
.		.	.	.
.		.	.	.
i.	$13,500	i	i	i
j.	I don't know	j	j	j
Miles per gallon				
a.	25	a	a	a
.		.	.	.
.		.	.	.
e.	45	e	e	e
f.	I don't know	f	f	f
Warranty period				
a.	12 months; 12,000 miles	a	a	a
.		.	.	.
.		.	.	.
h.	60 months; 60,000 miles	h	h	h
e.	I don't know	3	3	e
Ride comfort				
a.	soft/smooth	a	a	a
b.	soft/stiff	b	b	b
c.	springy/smooth	c	c	c
d.	springy/stiff	d	d	d
e.	I don't know	e	e	e

Figure 3.1: Examples of Product Positioning Questions

If attribute levels are complicated, require considerable verbal description, or are otherwise troublesome, one may need additional exploratory or prescaling work to produce levels that are meaningful and have sufficient variation to meet the objectives of the research.

Once levels are determined, product-positioning data can be obtained in a relatively direct manner (in product classes for which this makes sense): Individuals can be asked which level of each determinant decision attribute most closely matches their beliefs about those brands with which they are familiar. This resembles a multiple choice test in which consumers choose the level of each determinant decision attribute that comes closest to what they believe to be the "true" level of that attribute for each brand. Few individuals know all brands; hence one normally asks about brands which subjects know enough about to express an opinion. For example, for Japanese compact autos, one might ask the questions in Figure 3.1 about the attributes gasoline mileage, price, warranty, and ride.

Individuals' responses to questions like those in Figure 3.1 are measures of their beliefs or S_{jk}'s. We call these product-positioning measures because one can "position" each brand on each attribute in a perceptual (or belief) space. It usually is unwise to assume that consumers know the "true" physical attribute levels or the levels described in marketing communications or promotional literature. Also, for some product classes such as financial institutions, many individuals seem to have limited comparative knowledge; hence it may be difficult to obtain reliable product-positioning data.

Positioning data provide the initial conditions upon which to base behavioral change forecasts (discussed in Chapter 4) because the units of measurement of conjoint models ordinarily are belief or perceptual variables (S_k's). The mapping of physical variables into perceptual variables assumed by equation 1.1 may not be easy to develop or estimate. Thus, even if the mappings of equation 1.1 cannot be specified, one can obtain valuable and actionable information for formulating and evaluating strategy and tactics from product-positioning measures of attributes. If one wishes to use product-positioning measures in conjoint measures, the attribute levels in the positioning study must be the same as those in the conjoint experiment(s). Examples in which product-positioning data are used with conjoint models are given in Section 3.3.

3.4 Practical Approaches to Solving Conjoint Problems

This section discusses the design, implementation, and analysis of practical conjoint field research projects. Practical considerations often motivate one to sacrifice some theoretical and methodological niceties discussed in Chapters 1 and 2. Hence this chapter moves away from the ideal research situations of academic laboratories and other controlled situations to focus on expedient methods that "work." Practicality frequently requires one to make assumptions and/or tolerate some bias in order to obtain useful results.

3.4.1 PRACTICAL CONSIDERATIONS IN APPLYING
CONJOINT METHODS IN FIELD RESEARCH SETTINGS

3.4.1.1 Considerations Related to Tasks and Their Administration.
Factorial experiments and multiple replications discussed in Chapters 1
and 2 often can be used in academic research settings, but rarely can be
used in applied settings. Thus one normally has to make tradeoffs to
obtain practical results. For example, it usually is not possible to obtain
replications in field research unless consumers are well-compensated.
Thus one sacrifices statistical tests on individuals to obtain statistical
tests on groups. As the object of a conjoint study is normally to project
to some population of interest, this tradeoff rarely is problematic.

Although interest usually focuses on groups of individuals in applied
research, there are instances in which individuals are of interest. Some
examples include the development of expert systems, sophisticated
Delphi panel studies, and problems of sufficient importance to justify
studying single individuals, such as purchases of complicated and
expensive products and equipment. In the latter case, considerable time,
effort, and money often are invested to consummate a sale with one or a
small group of individuals; hence one might be motivated to understand
the decision processes of individuals involved in making the final purchase decision. Nonetheless, one is rarely interested in individuals per se;
rather, one is usually interested in populations.

A number of additional considerations in field studies can influence
one's results and therefore deserve mention. These include how one
explains the task to the subjects, types of category rating scales and their
meaning, and task format. Failure to give these considerations proper
attention may increase nonsampling error, leading to bias; hence let us
briefly consider each.

All conjoint tasks require a set of instructions in which the nature of
the task and the response scale are explained to subjects. One should
make the instructions simple and straightforward. Because all subjects
receive the instructions, they should be uniformly administered to avoid
differences in interpretation. One should tell subjects exactly what the
task is about and why, give them examples of attribute combinations,
show them how the response scale is to be used, and tell them why one
wants or needs their response information.

The primary considerations in choice of a rating scale are (a) a
sufficient number of categories for subjects to discriminate among the
treatments, (b) numbering or labeling of categories that does not invite
subjects to collapse them to a smaller number (e.g., 100 category scales

are often collapsed into 20 or fewer categories), (c) a response dimension that is meaningful to the research objective(s) (e.g., "satisfaction" may be unrelated to "purchase probability"), and (d) a description of the scale, its use, and its meaning that tells subjects how to use it and makes it easy for them to respond meaningfully.

The latter consideration often dictates labeling the ends and intermediate points of scales, providing convenient boxes to check, and the like. Although 5-category scales are common in marketing research, we rarely use them in applied work because there are insufficient categories for subjects to discriminate among the treatments. Instead, we often use scales with 11 or more categories, the number of categories being determined by the number of treatments. We use 11-category scales if there are 16 or fewer treatments; we use 21-category scales for larger designs.

The results of a conjoint study can be biased by learning effects. In particular, subjects tend to use the first few treatments to learn a task and develop a decision strategy. To reduce learning bias one should give subjects examples of how to do the task in the instructions, provide them with bounds on the range of attribute combinations (if possible), and place three to six treatments at the beginning of the task so that subjects will use them to learn how to do the task. However, if subjects are told the first few treatments are "practice," they may not take the task seriously.

Practice treatments should consist of a mix of all attribute levels; and, if possible, each attribute level should occur an equal number of times. Meyer (1977) demonstrated that subjects' decision strategies stabilize after three treatments in a three-attribute task. However, as the number of attributes increases, it is likely that the number of treatments used to learn a task increases; hence one should adjust the number of practice treatments accordingly. The order of the remaining treatments of primary experimental interest should be randomized; and, if possible, each subject should receive a different ordering. If this is not possible, several different orderings should be used to minimize order effects.

If one suspects that subjects may not use a rating scale in an equal-interval manner, one can take other precautions, including the use of "end-anchors," which are treatment combinations that define the ends of the scale, and "fillers," which are treatments that are slightly more extreme than the most extreme treatments. Unfortunately, one can use such tactics only if one knows that all subjects will agree on the extremes. Although one should use end-anchors and practice treatments whenever possible; fillers are rarely used outside of academic settings.

Having dealt with considerations related to the task and its administration, we now turn our attention to practical matters of design and analysis.

3.4.1.2 Practical Approaches to Approximating the Overall Utility Function (Equation 1.3).

3.4.1.2 Practical Approaches to Approximating the Overall Utility Function (Equation 1.3). The key mapping of interest in conjoint experiments is the specification of the overall utility function (equation 1.3). This mapping approximates an individual's decision process and allows one to estimate the relationship between positioning measures and utilities (equations 1.2 and 1.3). The key issues in approximating the overall value or utility function are the following:

(1) Are there nonlinear relationships between the determinant attributes and the individual's overall responses?
(2) Are there nonadditivities or interactions among the determinant attributes that significantly influence the variation in the individual's responses?
(3) Are there significant differences in the way different individuals or different groups of individuals respond to the determinant attributes? That is, can market segments be identified that are similar in their responses to the conjoint treatments?

Answers to these questions determine which of a number of possible design and analysis approaches should be considered in a particular case. In general, however, using two levels for attributes is often sufficient to meet one's objectives in practical research. Let us turn our attention to ways in which we can simplify conjoint problems by using linear functions to approximate more complicated decision functions that might be used by consumers.

3.4.1.3 Simplifying Conjoint Models by Assuming Responses to Be Approximately Linear. There are several ways to deal with the problem of nonlinearities in conjoint models; however, judging from published reports (see, e.g., Green and Srinivasan, 1978; Cattin and Wittink, 1982), it is common to restrict attributes to two levels. Although one cannot detect nonlinearities, designs are available for up to 30 or more attributes if one restricts attributes to two levels. For example, efficient, orthogonal main effects designs with sufficiently few treatments to be administered to single subjects are cataloged in Hahn and Shapiro (1966), Hedayat and Wallis (1978), and McLean and Anderson (1984). Thus a wide variety of designs exists to permit one to estimate main effects of two-level factors. Single subjects rarely are asked to judge more than 32 treatments in field situations unless offered a considerable incentive(s).

Because designs for two-level attributes do not permit nonlinearities to be estimated, they can be thought of as "end-point" designs. That is, the response effects can be estimated only at the extreme points in multiattribute space because no intermediate points are observed. Also, the results may depend upon whether nonadditivities are taken into account; hence it is often prudent to use designs that incorporate non-linearities and nonadditivities, even at the expense of some design and task complications.

3.4.1.4 Incorporating Nonlinearities and Nonadditivities in Conjoint Designs. If one wishes to estimate nonlinearities, there are many design possibilities, depending upon the number of levels of the attributes. Few practical research projects use more than three or four attribute levels to estimate nonlinearities; hence candidate designs are combinations of two-, three-, and four-level attributes. Hahn and Shapiro (1966), Chacko (1980), and McLean and Anderson (1984) contain catalogs of such designs. We now discuss design alternatives for practical research situations:

(1) "Main effects only" designs will provide estimates of nonlinearities for attributes with three or more levels, if all interactions are zero. This type of design is susceptible to confoundment bias due to unobserved interactions, hence it should be used only if one cannot use other designs. It is probably fair to say that such designs are used more often in applications than should be the case given that other options exist (see below).

(2) At a minimum, one should use "foldover" or "main effects + selected interactions" designs. Foldover designs permit one to estimate main effects orthogonal to unobserved but significant two-way interactions, if other interactions are zero. "Main effects + selected interactions" designs provide estimates of nonlinearities for attributes with three or more levels, as well as some selected nonadditivities, if all other interactions are zero. One should pilot test such designs to identify attributes likely to have large effects, because often (but not always) such attributes will interact with one or more other attributes that also have large main effects.

Foldover designs can be created easily from most main effects plans. One can construct a foldover design for two-level main effects plans by replacing 0, 1 design codes in the main effects design with 1, 0 to create its foldover. For three-level factors one replaces the design codes 0, 1, 2 with the codes 2, 1, 0 (the middle level is unchanged). A four-level factor coded 0, 1, 2, 3 is coded 3, 2, 1, 0 to create its foldover. Thus foldover designs consist of both a base main effects plan and its foldover.

(3) Another design strategy for handling nonlinearities and nonadditivities often requires fewer treatment combinations than foldover designs and can reduce bias in the main effects due to unobserved interactions. This strategy relies on the fact that often most of the variance in significant interactions is explained by the linear-by-linear interaction components. One can exploit this by developing two designs: (a) a main effects design to estimate nonlinearities and (b) a two-level, end-points design to estimate linear-by-linear two-way interaction effects. Concatenating the two designs into a single design creates a "compromise" design. Both main effects and linear-by-linear two-way interaction effects can be estimated from such plans.

Although not orthogonal, and therefore not as efficient as orthogonal designs, compromise plans often are good designs. However, in order to make such a design, one must know the end-points (the "best" and "worst" attribute levels). Unfortunately, as previously discussed, it is often difficult to define the end-points of qualitative attributes in a way that applies to all respondents, particularly if individuals' preferences for the various levels differ. Similarly, consumers may respond in U-shaped or inverse U-shaped manners with respect to some quantitative attributes; that is, individuals may prefer intermediate levels of attributes (e.g., amount of sugar in tea) to either end-point over a certain quantitative range. Hence utility may be highest for intermediate levels and lowest for end-points. In either case, using the same end-points for everyone may produce very misleading results; and, therefore, attribute levels should be pretested if possible.

(4) Another approach is to prescale the attribute levels using unidimensional scaling procedures to try to infer nonlinearities a priori. For example, respondents might rate each level of each attribute on a category-rating scale similar to that in the conjoint task, assuming all other attributes are held constant. If respondents ratings of the attribute levels indicate that their end-points differ, one must create a different design for each respondent using their revealed end-points as the two levels.

If respondents' response orderings for the end-points do not differ, one can use the same two-level end-point design for all. Once a respondent's part-worth utilities have been estimated, one can estimate the part-worth values of the unobserved levels of interest by using the prescaled levels as a basis for interpolation. Of course, unobserved significant interactions can bias the part-worth estimates; and it is unclear if unidimensional scales are reliable estimates of the part-worths estimated from conjoint tasks. Hence one should be cautious in using this approach.

(5) It is therefore often easier and wiser to develop a practical approach to estimate nonlinear main effects and two-way interactions from the outset. Frequently this can be done by creating within-subjects main effects plans that aggregate to permit tests of interactions between subjects. That is, one can "block" the overall design into sets of main effects plans. If one randomly assigns subjects into separate main effects designs (blocks), the rating data can be aggregated over blocks of subjects to permit tests of interaction effects. Aggregate tests require one to assume that the form and coefficients of the interaction effects are the same for all subjects, although the main effects can differ. This assumption can be relaxed somewhat, if one clusters the subjects according to similarities in main effects parameters and estimates the interaction effects separately for each cluster.

Once a design is chosen for a particular conjoint problem, one must consider statistical alternatives for approximating a subject's decision process as revealed by his or her response data. Alternative modeling possibilities are considered in the next section.

3.4.1.5 Developing Approximations to Nonlinear and Nonadditive Conjoint Models. Approximating the main and interaction effects of three- (four-) level attributes requires two (three) degrees of freedom for each main effect; and four (nine) degrees of freedom for each interaction. These interaction or cross-products can be viewed in an algebraic product sense as (a) the linear component of Attribute A times the linear component of Attribute B, (b) the linear of A times the quadratic of B, (c) the quadratic of A times the linear of B, and (d) the quadratic of A times the quadratic of B. Similarly, each main effect also can be described in terms of linear and quadratic components. In the case of four-level attributes, linear, quadratic, and cubic components are needed to describe both main and interaction effects completely.

Thus multiple polynomial linear regression analysis can be used to approximate individuals' responses to conjoint tasks. Regression approximations to respondents' response surfaces can be estimated by using orthogonal polynomial design codes in place of the actual levels of attributes to estimate the regression coefficients (see Figure 3.2). Without orthogonal codes, linear and squared terms are not independent; and, in fact, can be highly correlated. If one uses small designs with only a few treatments, such correlations can cause round-off errors in matrix inversion algorithms. Orthogonal polynomial codes ensure that statistical results are minimally affected by such problems.

Orthogonal polynomial codes for attributes with two to six levels are given in Figure 3.2. These codes can be thought of as different dummy codes that partition the variation in the response due to the levels of the attributes in a different way. Unlike (1, 0) dummies or effects codes, vectors of orthogonal polynomial codes are exactly orthogonal to one another and all estimable cross-products (interactions) if the original design matrix is orthogonal.

Linear and quadratic terms in regression models allow one to approximate conjoint response surfaces because, as demonstrated by Dawes and Corrigan (1974) and others, in most cases individuals' responses are monotonically related to the levels of each attribute, or the levels can be prescaled or rescaled to satisfy this condition. Thus second-degree polynomial approximations ordinarily suffice. Similarly, the interaction effects of quantitative attributes often can be approximated by cross-products of the linear and quadratic components. Thus, even if quantitative attributes have more than three levels, quadratic response surfaces usually suffice.

3.4.1.6 Combining Individual-Level and Aggregate Conjoint Response Information. One normally tries to develop a design that permits as much of the response surface as possible to be estimated at the level of the single respondent. If all effects of interest cannot be estimated for a single respondent, one can block the design so that additional effects of interest can be estimated across blocks of subjects. Polynomial multiple regression models can be used to approximate the individual and aggregate response surfaces. Alternatively, parameters can be estimated from the respondents' marginal and interaction means.

One way to analyze response data from blocked designs is to estimate the main effects for each subject, using these estimates to calculate residuals from predictions for each subject. The interaction effects can be estimated from the residuals. If there are equal numbers of subjects in

Number		Codes for Various Polynomial Terms				
of Levels		Linear	Quadratic	Cubic	Quartic	Quintic
2	0	−1				
	1	+1				
3	0	−1	+1			
	1	0	−2			
	2	+1	+1			
4	0	−3	+1	−1		
	1	−1	−1	+3		
	2	+1	−1	−3		
	3	−3	+1	+1		
5	0	−2	+2	−1	+1	
	1	−1	−1	+2	−4	
	2	0	−2	0	+6	
	3	+1	−1	−2	−4	
	4	+2	+2	+1	+1	
6	0	−5	+5	−5	+1	−1
	1	−3	−1	+7	−3	+5
	2	−1	−4	+4	+2	−10
	3	+1	−4	−4	+2	+10
	4	+3	−1	−7	−3	−5
	5	+5	+5	+5	+1	+1

Figure 3.2: Orthogonal Polynomial Codes for Factors with Two to Six Levels

each block, the response means for each treatment combination calculated across all subjects in a particular block can be regressed against the main effects and two-way interactions to estimate the parameters of interest. If sample sizes are equal in each block, estimates are consistent and unbiased, but standard errors are unreliable (inefficient). If sample sizes differ in each block, the latter approach produces inconsistent, biased, and inefficient estimates. Thus the analysis of response data from blocked designs is complicated because of the repeated measures aspect, which requires one to treat the data as a mixed time-series, cross-sectional problem.

If subjects are randomly assigned into the different blocks, parameters can be estimated for each subject in each block. The mean of each parameter and its associated standard error are estimated as described previously, although the parameters in each block are different linear combinations of unestimated interactions. If equal numbers of subjects are observed in each block, and all subjects share common interaction effects, the mean parameters are unbiased and consistent estimates of the main effects. The aggregate-level interaction estimates are consistent and unbiased, but all of the statistical tests of these interactions are inefficient.

Hence one can estimate the parameters of interest, but cannot rely upon the statistical tests. However, one ordinarily is interested in the estimates and their graphical representation, so this is a minor inconvenience in many applied problems. Furthermore, if one uses the graphical information and conducts sensitivity tests on the estimated parameters, one often can generalize about the effects despite the bias in the standard errors. As a rule of thumb, tests of the main effects are based on inflated standard errors because of the variability between blocks, while tests on the interactions are deflated by the lack of variability in the effects between subjects.

Let us consider design possibilities for three- and four-level attributes and for mixtures of two-, three-, and four-level attributes. For three-level factors, one can develop orthogonal, balanced main effects plans for the following practical situations: (a) The effects of up to 4 attributes can be estimated from 9 treatments, (b) up to 7 attributes from 18 treatments, and (c) up to 13 attributes from 27 treatments. Rarely are larger designs required. A number of selected two-factor interactions can be estimated from 27 treatments if there are 6 or fewer attributes. Additional interactions can be accommodated by merging a main effects plan for three-level attributes with a design that permits one to estimate all two-way interactions for the end-points using the two extreme levels of the attributes, creating a "compromise plan."

The remainder of this chapter describes a number of examples of applications of conjoint techniques to practical problems. These example applications illustrate the theory and the methods of implementation and analysis discussed in this and previous chapters.

3.5 Examples of Previous Applications of Conjoint Models to Practical Problems

3.5.1 CONSUMER EVALUATIONS OF PUBLIC BUS OPTIONS

In a 1971 study sponsored by the U.S. Department of Transportation (Louviere et al., 1973; Norman and Louviere, 1974), three attributes of public bus services were varied in a 3^3 factorial design to produce different "bus systems." Buses were described by fare (three levels: $0.15, $0.25, $0.35); service frequency (three levels: 15, 30, 60 minutes); and walking distance to the bus stop from home (three levels: 1/2, 3, 9 blocks). Subjects were paid University of Iowa student volunteers; each completed 12 replications of the design.

The order of treatments and of factors within treatments was randomized separately for each subject and replication. Subjects rated each treatment combination by making a slash mark on a 150-millimeter line scale labeled at either end by "definitely would never use this bus" and "definitely would always use this bus." Ratings were recorded to the nearest millimeter and assumed to be interval measures. Analysis of variance was used to analyze both individual subjects and the group of subjects as a whole.

Individual subject results suggested that each treated the attributes as complements; and therefore, a multiplicative model was a good approximation to the data. The multiplicative diagnosis was based on theory and methods explained in Chapter 2: All two- and three-way interactions were significant, and all displayed a convergent graphical form for undesirable attribute levels and a divergent form for desirable levels, indicating that subjects treated all of the attributes as complements.

A new bus system was introduced soon after the conjoint study, replacing poor service with good service. Results of the conjoint study were consistent with the performance of both systems: The old system had a 25 cent fare, 60-minute frequency of service, and poor route coverage. The new system had a 15 cent fare, many routes had 15-minute service, and many residences were within two blocks of a bus stop. The old system had very low ridership, while the new system had high ridership.

Additional studies of consumer evaluations of public transport systems have repeatedly supported the conclusion that consumers treat the attributes of these systems as complements. Furthermore, a number of studies have reported excellent correspondence between the predictions of conjoint models and individuals' mode choice behavior. Some of these studies include Louviere et al. (1974); Levin and Herring (1981); Louviere et al. (1981); Meyer et al. (1978); Norman (1977); Louviere and Kocur (1983); Kocur et al. (1982); and Bradley and Bovy (1985).

3.5.2 EVALUATIONS OF TOWNS AS POSSIBLE RESIDENTIAL SITES

Lerman and Louviere (1978) studied the residential choice behavior of workers in U.S. Rocky Mountain states in which there was considerable resource development activity requiring importation of skilled laborers both to develop sites and to operate them once developed.

There were few large towns in the study region, and workers rarely were able to live at rural work sites. Thus workers had to choose among residential options that differed in driving time and/or distance, town size, and amenities offered.

Lerman and Louviere (1978) conceptualized the workers' decision problem as a trade-off between town size and associated urban amenities, and the commuting distance to and from work. U.S. Census of Business data were used to estimate linear regression models to predict the number of facilities expected to be in various retail business classes (e.g., supermarkets, gas stations, and pharmacies), based on six town population sizes ranging from 250 to 25,000. The predicted number of facilities was used to create six levels of the composite variable "population plus associated amenities" such that population and each urban amenity were perfectly linearly related. A range of six driving-distance levels (5 to 150 miles) was used to reflect existing driving conditions; a 6×6 factorial design was created to vary the town and commuting distance descriptions.

Subjects were instructed to assume that they were employed at a rural resource site but could not live there, and were asked to rate the 36 town-and commuting-distance combinations as potential places to live on a 150-millimeter line mark scale. The rating scale was labeled at either end with the phrases, "definitely would not like to live here" or "definitely would like to live here." Subjects were a convenience sample of 75 faculty, students and staff from the University of Wyoming familiar with the problem faced by rural workers in Wyoming. A between and within analysis of variance revealed a very significant interaction between town size and commuting distance, consistent with a multiplicative or complementary relationship between the two attributes. Based on this diagnosis, a nonlinear multiplicative conjoint model was fit to the aggregate data.

Validation data were available from a U.S. Commerce Department survey of nonlocal workers employed at several rural locations in the U.S. West: the proportion of nonlocal workers who chose to reside in each local town and the driving distance from each local town to the employment sites. These data permitted Lerman and Louviere to test the conjoint model on a parallel set of real-world data. Louviere and Piccolo (1977) reported a significant Pearson rank-order correlation (0.92) between the mean rating responses predicted by the conjoint model and the choices observed in the U.S. Commerce Department survey data. This finding suggested that the survey data could be approximated by a statistical choice model specified in a similar way to the equation derived from the conjoint data. Multinomial logit choice models were fit to the survey data using 27 different utility specifications for town size and driving distance, chosen because they were consistent with (a) utility maximization and (b) what would be likely to occur to an applied econometrician. Each of the 27 specifications was compared statistically to the specification derived from the conjoint study, and all were found to be statistically inferior to that specification. Lerman and Louviere suggested that the conjoint specification probably would not have been used by an econometrician without the conjoint results. Thus the conjoint study provided information that not only enhanced the predictive power of an econometric choice model, but this information probably could not have been obtained in any other way.

3.5.3 CONSUMER CHOICES
AMONG COMPETING SUPERMARKETS

Louviere and Meyer (1981) studied the supermarket choices of residents of Tallahassee, Florida, and Laramie, Wyoming. In all, 100 individuals in both cities were interviewed by phone about reasons for choosing or not choosing supermarkets. Consumers in these semistructured interviews overwhelmingly stated that prices, selection, and convenience were the key decision attributes. These attributes were assigned three levels (above average, average, below average) and varied in a 3^3 conjoint experiment. A convenience sample of college students who were regular shoppers rated three replications of the 3^3 factorial on a 150-millimeter line mark scale. The ends of the scale were labeled "very good supermarket" or "very bad supermarket." Results suggested a multiplicative (complementary) conjoint model was a good approximation to the aggregate response data.

Next, 100 consumers were randomly sampled from phone directories in each city and personally interviewed to obtain supermarket positions (13 in Tallahassee, 5 in Laramie) on the levels of the three attributes used in the experiment. Trained graduate students counted patrons entering each supermarket in Tallahassee during a randomly chosen two-hour period of a randomly chosen day to provide external market choice data. In Laramie, a local expert provided gross annual sales estimates for each supermarket.

The positioning data were used in the aggregate conjoint model to predict the expected rating responses of the individuals in the positioning study. The predicted responses were graphed against the observed external market choice measures. In both cities a monotonic relationship was found, consistent with the multinomial logit choice model.

These results suggest that conjoint models can be used with product-positioning data to forecast performance measures such as market share, sales, and demand. Timmermans (1982) replicated the Louviere and Meyer (1981) findings for shopping center choice in the Netherlands, providing additional external validity evidence.

3.5.4 CONSUMER HOUSING PREFERENCES

Louviere (1979) reported two studies of consumers' preferences for housing alternatives: (a) 11 housing attributes, such as asking price, number of baths, and bedrooms, were varied in a 3^{11} main effects plan, and (b) additional housing attributes were varied with a $2^4 \times 3^9$ main effects plan. Subjects were random samples of residents of Laramie, Wyoming-who rated 27 (first study) or 36 (second study) housing descriptions on a 20-category rating scale.

In the second study, standardized and unstandardized regression coefficients were estimated for each subject. Standardized regression coefficients are equal to the simple correlations of the attributes with the response measure if a design is orthogonal. The partial R-squared of each attribute measures its relative impact on the responses. A MANOVA analysis was used to identify reliable associations between individual sociodemographic measures and the standardized and unstandardized regression parameters.

The preceding examples illustrate that conjoint analysis methods can be applied to many practical consumer decision problems. The next chapter will discuss how to use individual conjoint models to forecast choice behavior; and how to design controlled experiments to study choice behavior directly, rather than trying to draw inferences about choice behavior from the results of judgment tasks that do not require individuals to make choices from competing sets of alternatives.

4. PREDICTING LIKELY MARKET CHOICES FROM CONJOINT STUDIES AND OTHER STRATEGIC APPLICATIONS OF CONJOINT MODELS

4.0 Introduction

In this chapter we discuss ways to use conjoint data and models to derive strategic results for aggregate- and segment-level choice outcomes. Strategic and tactical market performance measures, such as market share and total demand, are the aggregate result of many individual choice decisions. Thus simulating consumer choices can provide insights into strategic marketing and management problems such as the analysis of competitive strategy and tactics, positioning and repositioning, pricing strategy, concept testing, new product development, communications strategy, and many others.

4.1 Approaches to Simulating Aggregate Market Choices Based on Conjoint Data or Individual Conjoint Models

Often commercial conjoint analysis studies have as their objective the prediction of the expected choices of a sample in response to various marketing or management actions involving changes in the levels of determinant decision attributes. Typically, such commercial applications involve (a) estimating individual conjoint models using multiple linear regression or other estimation procedures, (b) grouping subjects with similar conjoint models, and (c) developing computer simulation algorithms to predict which of a set of competing attribute profiles individuals are likely to choose. This section discusses how such choice predictions can be made, including ways to (a) enhance understanding of aggregate market response surfaces, (b) forecast demand as well as market share, and (c) calibrate decision models to real market situations.

4.1.1 A TYPICAL APPROACH USED IN COMMERCIAL CONJOINT STUDIES TO SIMULATE LIKELY AGGREGATE CHOICES

To simulate aggregate choice behavior, part-worth utilities must be estimated for each individual in a sample using multiple linear regression or other estimation techniques (e.g., MONANOVA). Sets of attribute treatments are used to represent alternative product concepts or product positions for new or existing products that could compete with other existing or proposed new products. Thus management actions are represented by treatments consisting of various combinations of levels of attributes varied in a conjoint experiment(s). The objective is to forecast the market share that each treatment is likely to capture in various competitive scenarios of interest to management.

Conjoint choice simulations require one to assume that management effectively communicates the attribute information about the brand(s) to the market and the market "believes" this information. Management usually wants to study a number of different competitive situations involving both their and competitors' products. Each competitive situation contains several competing attribute combinations and typically involves several competitive scenarios (see Green et al., 1981). For each competitive scenario of interest a computer program must be written to do the following:

(1) Predict the expected numerical response (overall utility) of each individual to each treatment combination in each competitive scenario. These predictions are made by substituting appropriately coded attribute levels for particular treatment combinations into each individual's conjoint model and estimating his or her expected response to that treatment.

(2) Identify the "best" treatment for each individual in each competitive scenario. *Best* is usually defined to be that treatment combination that receives the highest predicted utility in a particular competitive scenario, assuming that *higher* means more utility. Thus best is defined relative to the other treatments in a particular competitive scenario, not the best treatment over all scenarios.

(3) Predict the most likely choice of each individual in each competitive scenario, and assume it to be the most likely choice of that individual in that scenario. The computer program "counts" the predicted choices in Steps 1 to 3 for all treatment combinations in each competitive scenario. The expected market share of a treatment combination in a competitive scenario is estimated to be the total number of individuals for whom that treatment combination is predicted to be the best divided by the total number of individuals.

There are some variations in this approach: Sometimes it is assumed that the predicted responses (the expected overall utilities) are estimates of the parameters of particular choice models. For example, the Luce (1959, 1977) choice axiom or the multinomial logit choice model (McFadden, 1974, 1981; Hensher and Johnson, 1980; Manski and McFadden, 1981; Ben-Akiva and Lerman, 1985) often are assumed. Such assumptions have no empirical or theoretical support; hence they are ad hoc (e.g., Green et al., 1981: 23). Of course, the "best equals most likely first choice" assumption is also ad hoc. In the case of the multinomial logit model, the overall utility values predicted by an individual's conjoint model are assumed to be the expected values of the extreme value type I distribution, and the standard error of the regression is assumed to be the variance of that distribution. If this assumption is approximately correct, the probability that a particular predicted value is best (namely, "highest") can be determined from the multinomial logit model. In any case, if one accepts such assumptions, one proceeds as follows:

(1) The expected response of each individual to each treatment combination in a particular competitive scenario of management interest is computed.

(2) Instead of identifying the best predicted response, the predicted responses are assumed to be estimates of the parameters of the Luce choice axiom or the multinomial logit (MNL) model. These parameter estimates (the predicted responses) are used to predict the *probability* that an individual will choose a particular treatment combination (the i-th combination) in a particular competitive scenario (i & others). For example,

P(choosing i|i & others) = U(i)/[U(a) + U(b) + . . . + U(i) + . . . + U(J)]
(Luce axiom)

P(choosing i|i & others) = exp[U(i)]/{exp[U(a)] + . . . + exp[U(J)]}
(Multinomial Logit Model).

U(x) refers to the overall utilities that are observed or estimated. The ratings responses predicted by an individual's conjoint model (e.g., a regression equation) are estimates of U(x), while ratings assigned by individuals to existing products or to a nonpurchase option are the observed (x). These latter ratings are not predicted by an individual's conjoint model, they are observed in a survey (see Section 4.1.2).

(3) The predicted probabilities for a particular treatment combination in a particular competitive scenario are summed over all the sample individuals to generate the expected market share for that treatment in that scenario.

(4) The first three steps are repeated for each competitive scenario of interest.

Louviere and Woodworth (1983) and Louviere (1988) compared the "choice-equals-best" approach with the assumption that the predicted utilities satisfy the scale value assumptions of the MNL model in a study of the retirement destination choices of a random sample of 327 Iowans aged 55-65. Unlike most commercial simulation efforts, the competitive scenarios were based on a designed experiment that satisfies the necessary and sufficient conditions to estimate MNL choice models. As explained in Section 4.2 (see also Louviere and Woodworth, 1983), the basic idea is to jointly design both the attribute treatments and the competitive scenarios in which they appear so that the joint design satisfies the statistical assumptions of particular choice models like the MNL model.

The use of an experimental design that satisfies the assumptions of the MNL model enables one to estimate the MNL parameters in an efficient manner from the simulated aggregate choices of the sample. MNL parameters were estimated from the choice data generated by two methods of simulating choices (a) "best predicted value equals choice" and (b) predicted conjoint responses used as estimates of MNL parameters. No significant differences were found in the two sets of parameters: however, further research is needed to generalize this finding to other product classes or simulation problems.

4.1.2 ENHANCEMENTS TO CONJOINT CHOICE SIMULATORS

4.1.2.1 Developing Controlled Experiments to Vary Choice Options and Competitive Scenarios. The use of controlled choice experiments that satisfy the assumptions of the MNL choice model to develop competitive scenarios is one way to enhance choice simulators (Louviere and Woodworth, 1983; Louviere, forthcoming). That is, in addition to or as part of the competitive scenarios of management interest, a simulation algorithm can be used to predict the expected choices of the sample in a set of statistically designed competitive scenarios. As explained in Section 4.2, competitive scenarios are termed *choice sets*; and each choice set consists of a different combination of competing attribute combinations.

To implement this approach, one develops an algorithm to predict the number of individuals expected to choose each treatment combination and/or choice option in each choice set. The predicted aggregate choice frequencies are analyzed statistically to estimate the parameters of a MNL choice model. The estimated MNL model describes the behavior of the aggregate (market or segment) choice surface and can be used to forecast the expected aggregate choices of the sample for any competitive scenario of interest. This approach is not limited to the MNL model; one also can design choice simulations to estimate the parameters of other choice models.

Most choice simulations performed to date have had the objective of predicting the probability of choosing a particular treatment combination given that it competes with other treatment combinations. This is equivalent to predicting the expected choice of an individual, given that he or she will make a choice. In many product markets, however, consumers may choose not to purchase; and, therefore, predictions of the expected market shares in a particular competitive scenario may be erroneous because individuals are counted as "purchasers" who are unlikely to purchase.

4.1.2.2 Including Existing Brands and the Nonpurchase Option in Choice Simulators. Existing products and/or a nonpurchase option can be included in a choice simulator by having individuals rate them as part of a conjoint task. These ratings can be incorporated into choice simulators by comparing the predicted rating responses to treatment combinations with ratings of a nonpurchase option and/or brands already in the market. Ratings of existing brands and/or a nonpurchase option are likely to have higher (i.e., "better") ratings than many of the treatments in the competitive scenarios; hence they should be more likely to be chosen. For example, Louviere (1988) reports that respondent ratings of their present residential situation as a retirement migration destination opportunity are higher than the ratings predicted for almost all conjoint treatments describing retirement options. Because only a small proportion of elderly retirees actually leave their present residence, adjusting a choice simulator to account for staying in one's present residence produces more realistic forecasts.

The advantages of incorporating brand and/or nonpurchase ratings in choice simulators are (a) competitive strengths of existing brands can be assessed; (b) competitive strengths of different attribute combinations (e.g., new product concepts or repositionings of existing products) can be assessed in competition with existing brands; and (c) demand estimates can be generated if a nonpurchase alternative is used in the simulations.

4.1.2.3 Calibrating Conjoint Model Predictions to Existing Choices. Conjoint models or models of choice simulators can be calibrated to current choices of consumers. For example, one can observe individuals' recent choice behavior (e.g., last item purchased, approximate proportion of total choices allocated to each brand in last x months, approximate dollars spent on each brand in the past x months, brand with most dollars allocated to it over the past six months). This choice information can be combined with positioning information to predict an individual's or a group's expected response to that combination of levels: For example, individuals can be asked to position familiar brands (the "evoked set") on the levels of the attributes (see Section 3.1.3 and Figure 3.1).

The expected responses can be used as the explanatory variable in a MNL model to be estimated from the observed choice data. One also can use conjoint models representing the aggregate market or particular market segments to generate individuals' expected ratings; these predicted ratings can be calibrated to individuals' observed choices using a MNL model. One also can use a MNL model estimated from a controlled choice simulation to predict the expected utilities of individuals' choices, using the vector of expected utilities as the explanatory variable in a MNL model to be estimated from the individuals' observed choices. Such calibration procedures are ad hoc, but provide a way to maximize external validity by relating the output of conjoint models directly to observed choice behavior. Such calibration procedures are analogous to the calibration of preference judgments to laboratory test market choices used in models like ASSESSOR (Urban and Hauser, 1980).

An example of calibrating conjoint model predictions to observed choice data is given by Kocur et al. (1982). Kocur et al. used a multinomial logit model to calibrate the predicted rating responses of a large sample (almost 50,000) of Wisconsin residents to reported mode, destination, and route choices. The results were used to develop a system of integrated statewide travel-choice-forecasting models for the Department of Transportation of the State of Wisconsin.

Louviere and Kocur (1983) calibrated the predicted responses of a sample of 1978 residents of Xenia, Ohio, to the attributes of six transit systems that were supported by federal funds after a disastrous tornado in 1974. Louviere and Kocur found that backcasts of choices based on conjoint models tracked the observed changes in patronage responses to the six different services.

4.1.2.4 An Expedient Method for Developing Choice Models from Conjoint Ratings Data. Disadvantages of conjoint simulation methods include time and cost to implement and apply and difficulty explaining the process to management. Because individual data are stored in computer files and constantly manipulated, choice simulators often perform poorly on microcomputers. A simple, but crude, method for forecasting the expected choices of consumers based on their observed rating data alone might be considered in lieu of a simulation.

This approach uses individuals' ratings to estimate the probability that a particular treatment, existing product, or nonpurchase option is a "high utility" alternative. The number of ratings in the sample (or in subsegments of the sample) that exceed an arbitrary category value are counted; and this count is used to estimate the distribution of "high" utilities for each treatment. For example, if individuals rate treatments on a 0-10 category scale, one can count the number of 10s, or the number of ratings of 7 or higher given to each treatment. The counts provide an estimate of the binomial outcome: "high" versus "not high" utility.

The "high" ratings frequencies associated with each treatment contain sufficient statistical information to estimate the parameters of a binary logit model, which can be written as follows:

$$p(a = \text{"high"}) = \exp[U(a)]/\{\exp[U(a)] + \exp[U(\text{"not high"})]\} \qquad [4.3]$$

where

p(a = "high") is the probability of rating treatment a equal to or greater than some arbitrary "high" rating.

U(a), U("not high") are the unknown overall utilities associated with saying treatment a is "high" vs. "not high."

exp is the symbol for exponentiation.

Equation 4.3 indicates that the denominator of the binary logit model is a constant for a particular treatment a. Thus, one can rewrite equation 4.3 as:

$$p(a = \text{"high"}) = \exp[U(a)]/K_a, \qquad [4.4]$$

where all terms are as previously defined, except for K_a, which is the denominator constant for the a-th treatment. Taking natural logarithms (Ln) of both sides of equation 4.4 yields

$$\text{Ln}[p(a = \text{"high"})] = U(a) - \text{Ln}(K_a), \qquad [4.5]$$

where all terms are as previously defined.

Equation 4.5 indicates that we can parameterize U(a) if we have estimates of p(a = "high") and p(a = "not high") (see also Louviere and Woodworth, 1983; Nakanishi and Cooper, 1982). Subjects' responses to the treatments in a conjoint experiment provide estimates of both probabilities. Hence one can parameterize U(a) as a linear-in-the-parameters-and-variables function of a design matrix corresponding to the treatment combinations. One uses the natural logarithm of the observed distribution of "high" ratings as the dependent variable in a generalized (weighted) least squares regression in which the observed rating frequencies for each treatment are the elements of the weighting vector. K_a is absorbed into the intercept. In this model the option of rating a as "not a high utility" treatment serves as the zero point on the utility scale.

If individuals rate existing products and/or a nonpurchase option, these alternatives can be scaled by using dummy variables to represent their effects. If one blocks treatments into different sets, one can also ask individuals to rate a common set of existing products and/or a nonpurchase option. Alternatively, a nonpurchase option could be used as the option against which each treatment is compared, and a binary logit or probit model could be used to represent the comparison data. The binary logit formulation for this comparison would be identical to equation 4.3, except that one would estimate the probability that treatment a was rated "higher" than the nonpurchase option.

Louviere (1982) applied this approximation to elderly housing and mobility choices: Respondents were assigned into one of five different blocks containing two 9-treatment main effects designs drawn from a 3^4. One main effects design in each block was used to study housing preferences and the other to study mobility preferences. The main effects designs aggregated to estimate all main effects and two-way interactions independently of one another and of unobserved but significant three-way interactions. A national sample of 1200 elderly individuals responded to the treatments on a 0-to-10 category rating scale.

The response frequency of each rating category was calculated for each treatment; and the distribution of these frequencies was used to estimate binary logit models that forecast the choices that the sample should make in response to changes in the attributes of housing and mobility options. Results for arbitrary combinations of rating categories (e.g., ratings of 9 and 10 compared with ratings of 7, 8, 9, and 10) suggested that binary logit model parameters (except intercept terms) were relatively insensitive to choice of arbitrary category grouping.

Additionally, Louviere et al. (1981) estimated binary logit models from the frequency distributions of ratings of arbitrary category groupings on both the negative and positive ends of rating scales. Logit parameters estimated from the negative category frequencies were mirror images of parameters estimated from positive category frequencies, which suggests this crude approximation is relatively insensitive to choice of rating category cutoff. Other binary outcome models, such as the probit model (Malhotra, 1983; Thurstone, 1927) also can be used to describe such ratings data. If one treats rating data as binary, one does not need to make metric assumptions about the response data as discussed in the previous chapters.

4.2 Integrating Conjoint and Discrete Choice Techniques to Study Choice Behavior Directly

Recent developments in the design and analysis of discrete choice experiments allow one to avoid developing individual-level decision models and/or using individual conjoint models to simulate choices. In particular, Louviere and Woodworth (1983), Louviere and Hensher (1982, 1983), and Louviere (1983, 1984a, 1986, 1988) discuss methods for the design and analysis of discrete choice experiments based on the MNL model and its generalizations. Discrete choice experiments permit one to model directly the choices that individuals make in various competitive scenarios (choice sets) without recourse to simulation algorithms and the assumptions involved.

Direct observation of the choices that individuals make in various competitive situations permits one to test various choice models. For example, the MNL model makes strong predictions about choice behavior that may not hold in real product markets; and one can design choice experiments to test these predictions. This capability also allows one to generalize MNL models if the experimental results suggest this to be necessary (see, e.g., McFadden, 1981; Batsell and Polking, 1985; Rotondo, 1986). Although violations of MNL model assumptions can be detected with experimentally designed choice simulations based on individual conjoint functions (Louviere and Woodworth, 1983; Louviere, 1988), it cannot be determined if such violations are the result of faulty assumptions programmed into the simulation or true departures reflecting important aspects of consumer choice behavior.

4.2.1 DESIGN AND ANALYSIS OF DISCRETE CHOICE EXPERIMENTS

4.2.1.1 Using 2^N Designs to Create Choice Sets and Fractional Designs to Create Offerings. To design discrete choice experiments one needs to develop two different experimental designs: (a) a design to create conjoint treatments (choice alternatives) of experimental interest and (b) a design to create choice sets into which to put the treatments that are to compete with one another. The design used to generate choice alternatives need not be an experimental design; in fact, it need only be a list of competing choice alternatives. Such a list might include all products or services competing in a particular product class or existing products and sets of conjoint treatments representing new product concepts that might be introduced.

The purpose of a choice-set-generating design is to assign the "list" of competing choice alternatives into different choice sets from which individuals will choose or perhaps allocate resources among (discussed later in this chapter). Choice-set-generating designs are used to assign the alternatives (treatments, existing products, and) to sets such that the assignment satisfies assumptions of various choice models such as the MNL model.

For example, consider the multinomial logit (MNL) model:

$$p(a \mid A) = \exp[U(a)] / \{\exp[U(a)] + \exp[U(b)] + \ldots + \exp[U(J)]\} \quad [4.6]$$

where

$p(a \mid A)$ is the probability of choosing alternative (treatment, existing brand, and so on) a from a choice set A in which a, b, ..., and J are members.

All other terms were previously defined, except $U(b)$ and $U(J)$, the utilities of alternatives b and J, respectively. Equation 4.6 indicates that a MNL model is completely defined by the unknown $U(x)$ parameters that define the marginal probabilities of choosing each alternative. Thus a necessary and sufficient condition for an experiment to satisfy the MNL model is to design it such that the marginals can be estimated independently of one another. Louviere and Woodworth (1983) demonstrate that this can be done with a 2^N design (N is the total number of choice alternatives on the list).

Let us use a simple experiment involving four competing brands (say A, B, C, and D) to explain why 2^N designs satisfy the assumptions of MNL models. The four brands are available or not, and as illustrated in Figure 4.1, there are 16 possible sets of choice sets given by a 2^4 factorial of "available or not." Each brand represents a factor with two levels

| | | Brands at the Local Retailer | | |
		A	B	C	D
Choice set	1	NA	NA	NA	NA
Choice set	2	NA	NA	NA	A
Choice set	3	NA	NA	A	NA
Choice set	4	NA	NA	A	A
Choice set	5	NA	A	NA	NA
Choice set	6	NA	A	NA	A
Choice set	7	NA	A	A	NA
Choice set	8	NA	A	A	A
Choice set	9	A	NA	NA	NA
Choice set	10	A	NA	NA	A
Choice set	11	A	NA	A	NA
Choice set	12	A	NA	A	A
Choice set	13	A	A	NA	NA
Choice set	14	A	A	NA	A
Choice set	15	A	A	A	NA
Choice set	16	A	A	A	A

NOTE: A = available (present in choice set); NA = not available (not present in choice set).

Figure 4.1: Illustration of a 2^N Choice Set Generating Design

("available or not available"), and the occurrences of "available" define what brands are in what choice sets. The main effects and interaction columns of a 2^N design are orthogonal; hence the number of times a brand is chosen given that it is available is an estimate of its marginal choice probability. If the main effects are orthogonal, the estimates of the marginals are independent, which satisfies the necessary and sufficient conditions of MNL models.

Because each cross-product or interaction is orthogonal, such factorial designs have additional, important statistical properties. In particular, the interaction effects represent joint choice probabilities; and if the MNL model is correct, these joint choice probabilities are completely determined by the marginal probabilities. These "interactions" must be zero in theory; and, if significant, disconfirm the simple MNL model, suggesting alternative choice models are more appropriate. Thus these interactions permit one to test the assumptions or deductions of various choice models such as the MNL model.

This concept of testing the MNL model is similar to testing various algebraic conjoint models in functional measurement. Thus one can test whether choice data satisfy a MNL model, and if they do not, one can generalize a MNL model by adding cross-product terms that represent differential effects of one alternative on another. That is, if the availability of brand A differentially affects brand B, the cross-product of A on B should be significantly larger than predicted by a MNL model. This generalization can be thought of as putting brand A into brand B's utility function (or brand B into A's Utility function). Similarly, one also can generalize a MNL model by including cross-effects of the attributes of each brand on other brands.

2^N-choice-set-generating designs can be used to estimate choice probabilities for the brands in Figure 4.1, which, in turn, can be used to estimate the parameters of various models of choice processes assumed to produce the choice data. For example, if one assumes that a multinomial logit choice model is a good approximation to one's choice data, one can use the MNL model to scale each brand, selecting one to be the origin of the scale. If each brand name can be scaled, it is (we hope) obvious that one also can scale alternatives that are treatment combinations instead of names.

For example, instead of the brand names in Figure 4.1, one can substitute attribute combinations drawn from a fractional factorial experiment as illustrated in Figure 4.2. Figure 4.2 contains (a) nine different treatments generated from a main effects, fractional factorial of a 3^4 and (b) a 2^9-choice-set-generating design used to place the nine treatments into choice sets based on a 16-treatment main effects + selected interactions design. The combined choice experiment is illustrated in Figure 4.2c.

Subjects evaluate the 15 choice sets illustrated in Figure 4.2c and choose one and only one of the treatments in each choice set as the one they "are most likely to purchase," "find the most attractive," and so on. The aggregate choice frequencies of the sample constitute empirical estimates of the unknown choice probabilities. Generalized least squares or maximum likelihood procedures can be applied to the choice frequencies to estimate the parameters of a MNL choice model. The overall utility values of the nine attribute combinations are a function of the design matrix representing the attribute levels used in the design. Hence one can estimate the part-worth utilities directly from a MNL analysis.

It is often convenient to set the origin of the utility scale by including an alternative in a choice design that is not one of the treatment combinations, but is a realistic choice option. We refer to such options as "base" alternatives; an obvious example of which is the option to

Design (a): Combinations of Levels of Four 3-Level Attributes Denoted 0, 1, and 2
(i.e., the choice alternatives)

Attributes	1	2	3	4	5	6	7	8	9	10
I	0	0	0	1	1	1	2	2	2	constant
II	0	1	2	0	1	2	0	1	2	constant
III	0	1	2	1	2	0	2	0	1	constant
IV	0	2	1	1	0	2	2	1	0	constant

Design (b): 2-to-the-9th Design to Put Design (a) Treatments into 16 Choice Sets
(0 denotes "available" and 1 denotes "not available)

Choice Set

1	0	0	1	0	0	1	1	1	1	1
2	0	0	1	0	1	0	1	0	0	1
3	0	0	1	1	0	0	0	1	0	1
4	0	0	1	1	1	1	0	0	1	1
5	0	1	0	0	0	1	1	0	0	1
6	0	1	0	0	1	0	1	1	1	1
7	0	1	0	1	0	0	0	0	1	1
8	0	1	0	1	1	1	0	1	0	1
9	1	0	0	0	0	1	0	1	0	1
10	1	0	0	0	1	0	0	0	1	1
11	1	0	0	1	0	0	1	1	1	1
12	1	0	0	1	1	1	1	0	0	1
13	1	1	1	0	0	1	0	0	1	1
14	1	1	1	0	1	0	0	1	0	1
15	1	1	1	1	0	0	1	0	0	1
16	1	1	1	1	1	1	1	1	1	1

(c) Choice Sets Shown to Subjects Based on Designs (a) and (b):
Treatments from Design (a)

Choice Set

1	3, 6, 7, 8, 9, 10 (constant base)
2	3, 5, 7, 10 (constant base)
3	3, 4, 8, 10 (constant base)
4	3, 4, 5, 6, 9, 10 (constant base)
5	2, 6, 7, 10 (constant base)
6	2, 5, 7, 8, 9, 10 (constant base)
7	2, 4, 9, 10 (constant base)
8	2, 4, 5, 6, 8, 10 (constant base)
9	1, 6, 8, 10 (constant base)
10	1, 5, 9, 10 (constant base)
11	1, 4, 7, 8, 9, 10 (constant base)
12	1, 4, 5, 6, 7, 10 (constant base)
13	1, 2, 3, 6, 9, 10 (constant base)
14	1, 2, 3, 5, 8, 10 (constant base)
15	1, 2, 3, 4, 7, 10 (constant base)
16	1,22, 3, 4, 5, 6, 7, 8, 9, 10 (constant base)

Figure 4.2: Construction of a Conjoint Choice Design

"choose no alternatives." One also might use "any other option not specifically mentioned," or one of the existing brands to set the origin of the utility scale.

The advantage of using a "base" option to set the origin of the utility scale can be seen if we rewrite the MNL model as follows:

$$Ln[p(a\,|\,A)] = Ln[p("base"\,|\,\overset{*}{A})] + [U(a) - U("base")], \qquad [4.7]$$

where all terms are as previously defined, except those involving the "base," or origin alternative. Equation 4.7 indicates that if the same "base" alternative is present in every choice set, it acts as a constant (zero) subtracted from the utilities of the other alternatives. Hence the design properties of the attribute treatments (e.g., orthogonality of attribute vectors) are unaffected unless the attribute levels of the base vary across choice sets. In the latter case the levels of the base must be subtracted from that of each alternative in each choice set, which changes the statistical properties of the attribute vectors (see, Mahajan, Green, and Goldberg, 1982). Hence use of a common "base" in all choice sets is recommended if possible.

The analysis of choice data from the experiment of Figure 4.2 is illustrated in Figure 4.3. The choice data are coded for generalized least squares estimation based on equation 4.5 (see also Louviere and Wood-worth, 1983). The coding in Figure 4.3 also can be used with other estimation procedures, such as iteratively reweighted least squares (Woodworth and Louviere, 1984), minimum chi-square (Bishop et al., 1975), or maximum likelihood (McFadden, 1974). One can use dummy variables to control for the denominator or base effects in each choice set (equations 4.5 and 4.7). Alternatively, some statistical estimation programs allow one to treat the denominators as a single categorical variable, the effects of which can be controlled without dummy variables.

A major advantage of choice experiments is that they address the primary objective of most conjoint studies—prediction of consumer choices. Because the choices of consumers can be observed directly, one does not have to make ad hoc assumptions to translate conjoint model predictions into choices, nor to design, develop, and implement choice simulation algorithms. One has control over the choice-set-generating design and the choice models that can be developed and tested. Hence one does not have to assume that consumers make choices in particular ways; rather, one can test various choice strategies (e.g., a MNL Choice

Choice Set (1-16)	Treatment (1-10)	Dependent Variable (frequency)	Attr I L0	Attr I L1	Attr II L0	Attr II L1	Attr III L0	Attr III L1	Attr IV L0	Attr IV L1
			— Coding of the Levels of the Attributes							
1	3	f3, 1	1	−1	−1	−1	−1	−1	−1	1
1	6	f6, 1	−1	1	−1	−1	1	−1	−1	−1
1	7	f7, 1	−1	−1	1	−1	−1	−1	−1	−1
1	8	f8, 1	−1	−1	−1	1	1	−1	−1	1
1	9	f9, 1	−1	−1	−1	−1	−1	1	1	−1
1	10	f10, 1	0	0	0	0	0	0	0	0
2	3	f3, 2	1	−1	−1	−1	−1	−1	−1	1
2	5	f5, 2	−1	1	−1	−1	−1	−1	1	−1
2	7	f5, 2	−1	−1	1	−1	−1	1	−1	1
2	10	f10, 2	0	0	0	0	0	0	0	0
3	3	f3, 3	1	−1	−1	−1	−1	−1	−1	1
3	4	f4, 3	−1	1	1	−1	−1	1	−1	1
3	8	f8, 3	−1	−1	−1	1	1	−1	−1	1
3	10	f10, 3	0	0	0	0	0	0	0	0
.	.	.	.		.		.		.	
.	.	.	.		.		.		.	
.	.	.	.		.		.		.	
.	.	.	.		.		.		.	
13	1	f1, 13	1	−1	1	−1	1	−1	1	−1
13	2	f2, 13	1	−1	−1	1	−1	1	−1	−1
13	3	f3, 13	1	−1	−1	−1	−1	−1	−1	1
13	6	f6, 13	−1	1	−1	−1	1	−1	−1	−1
13	9	f9, 13	−1	−1	−1	−1	−1	1	1	−1
13	10	f10, 13	0	0	0	0	0	0	0	0
.	.	.	.		.		.		.	
.	.	.	.		.		.		.	
.	.	.	.		.		.		.	
16	1	f1, 16	1	−1	1	−1	1	−1	1	−1
16	2	f2, 16	1	−1	−1	1	−1	1	−1	−1
16	3	f3, 16	1	−1	−1	−1	−1	−1	−1	1
16	4	f4, 16	−1	1	1	−1	−1	1	−1	1
16	5	f5, 16	−1	1	−1	1	−1	−1	1	−1
16	6	f6, 16	−1	1	−1	−1	1	−1	−1	−1
16	7	f7, 16	−1	−1	1	−1	−1	−1	−1	−1
16	8	f8, 16	−1	−1	−1	1	1	−1	−1	1
16	9	f9, 16	−1	−1	−1	−1	−1	1	1	−1
16	10	f10, 16	0	0	0	0	0	0	0	0

NOTE: The choice set indicator can be treated as 15 (1, 0) dummy variables (i.e., the observation is either in a particular choice set or not). fx, z is the number of choices observed for alternative (treatment combination) x in choice set number z. (−1, +1) dummy variables are used to code the attribute levels so that the base alternative will be exactly equal to the origin, as explained in the text. The utilities of the levels can be obtained from the following simple arithmetic: U (Level 0) = b (Level 0) × (+1) +b (Level 1) × (−1).

Figure 4.3: Analysis of Choice Data from Design in Figure 4.2

process), and if found to be inappropriate, one can estimate alternative model forms.

4.2.1.2 Other Designs for Choice Experiments. 2^N designs can be used to simulate out-of-stock or differences in availability conditions, create choice sets of different sizes, or test particular choice models. However, there are many other possible ways to design choice experiments, such as fixing the number of choice alternatives but varying the number of attributes that describe alternatives (Louviere and Woodworth, 1983). Such designs consist of a fixed number of brands, each described by one or more attributes; they can be generated in the following ways:

(1) Each brand can be described by a number of attributes, say M. If all brands have identical numbers of attributes and identical numbers of levels, one can create $n^M \times n^M \times \ldots \times n^M$ fractional factorial designs that satisfy the necessary and sufficient conditions for estimating MNL models. That is, if B brands have the same number of attributes (M), there are a total of BM attributes, each with n levels. A n^{BM} factorial can be used to generate choice sets in which the attributes of each brand are orthogonal, satisfying the condition that the marginals of each brand be independent.

If choice alternatives are specific, named brands, not generic attribute combinations, one may need brand-specific dummy variables to capture different brand effects. This is illustrated in Figure 4.4, in which a 3^4 effects plan is used to create nine different pricing scenarios (choice sets) for four different brands. The specific, named brands (Brands A-D) are offered at a different price in each choice set. Subjects choose one and only one brand in each choice set. A constant base alternative can be included in each choice set as well (e.g., purchasing none of the brands).

If the effects of the price variables in Figure 4.4 vary from brand to brand, one needs brand-specific price effects. One can test the significance of brand-specific price effects with a design like that in Figure 4.4. The analysis of such tests is illustrated in Figures 4.5a (brand-specific constants; generic price effects) and 4.5b (brand-specific constants; brand-specific price effects). Violations of the MNL model's assumption that only the marginal effects exist can also be tested by including the prices of other competing brands in each brand's utility function.

If one uses a constant base alternative in the experiment illustrated in Figure 4.4, one codes this alternative uniformly zero, except for a choice set indicator variable (or equivalent 1, 0 dummy variables to account

Choice Set	Brand A		Brand B		Brand C		Brand D	
	Design	Price ($)	Design	Price ($)	Design	Price ($)	Design	Price ($)
1	0	10	0	11	0	9	0	12
2	0	10	1	15	1	11	2	22
3	0	10	2	19	2	13	1	17
4	1	13	0	11	1	11	1	17
5	1	13	1	15	2	13	0	12
6	1	13	2	19	0	9	2	22
7	2	16	0	11	2	13	2	22
8	2	16	1	15	0	9	1	17
9	2	16	2	19	1	11	0	12

NOTE: The design used to generate the prices is the same main effects design that was used in Figure 4.2 to create the attribute combinations. Although the price levels used in this example are evenly spaced, one can use uneven spacing. The properties of this design are that each of the price columns is independent of the others. Thus one can estimate the marginals independently.

Figure 4.4: A Choice Experiment with Brand-Specific Effects

for the MNL model denominator "effects"). Attribute combinations (treatments) can be coded as one would code them in a conjoint regression analysis, with the following caveat: Parameter estimates for attributes coded (0, 1) can differ from estimates based on other codes (e.g., -1, +1) because (0, 1) codes define a contrast with the origin alternative, while (-1, +1) codes define a contrast between attribute levels that is not confounded with the origin. Furthermore, the origin may be considerably outside the range of the levels of numerical attributes, and if this is not taken into account in estimation, error may be introduced into the parameter estimation process. This problem can be minimized by using orthogonal polynomial codes for the levels of the numerical attributes, centering the levels of numerical attributes about their respective means or using (-1, +1) or other non (0, 1) dummies to code attribute levels. Finally, (-1, +1) codes minimize spurious collinearities in the design matrix, which can cause round-off errors in matrix inversion routines. This problem can be serious if one is dealing with small design matrices. (2) As the number of brands increases or the number of attributes within brands increases or both, the first design strategy produces increasingly larger numbers of choice sets. Alternative design strategies include (a) using the previous design strategy for all pairs of brands, (b) using a 2^B design to generate sets of brands and using the aforementioned design strategy to create separate designs for each set, or (c) generating attri-

Choice Set	Dependent Variable (frequency)	A	B	C	Generic Prices	Pr A	Pr B	Pr C	Pr D
						Brand-Specific Prices			

(a)   Coding the Design in Figure 4.4 for Analysis

Choice Set	Dependent Variable (frequency)	A	B	C	Generic Prices
1	fA,1	1	0	0	10
1	fB,1	0	1	0	11
1	fC,1	0	0	1	9
1	fD,1	0	0	0	12
2	fA,2	1	0	0	10
21	fB,2	0	1	0	15
2	fC,2	0	0	1	11
2	fD,2	0	0	0	22
.	.	.	.	.	.
.	.	.	.	.	.
.	.	.	.	.	.
9	fA,9	1	0	0	16
9	fB,9	0	1	0	19
9	fc,9	0	0	1	11
9	fD,9	0	0	0	12

(b)   Coding for Brand-Specific Dummies and Brand-Specific Prices

Choice Set	Dependent Variable (frequency)	A	B	C	Pr A	Pr B	Pr C	Pr D
1	fA,1	1	0	0	10	0	0	0
1	fB,1	0	1	0	0	11	0	0
1	fC,1	0	0	1	0	0	9	0
1	fD,1	0	0	0	0	0	0	12
2	fA,2	1	0	0	10	0	0	0
2	fB,2	0	1	0	0	15	0	0
2	fC,2	0	0	1	0	0	11	0
2	fD,2	0	0	0	0	0	0	22
.	.	.	.	.	.	.	.	.
.	.	.	.	.	.	.	.	.
.	.	.	.	.	.	.	.	.
9	fA,9	1	0	0	16	0	0	0
9	fB,9	0	1	0	0	19	0	0
9	fC,9	0	0	1	0	0	11	0
9	fD,9	0	0	0	0	0	0	12

NOTE: The choice set indicator column can be coded as 8 (1, 0) dummy variables to control for choice set denominator effects. Price levels can be dummy coded (-1, $+1$) if one wants to estimate the utilities for each level, instead of the numerical coding illustrated; however, if numerical coding is used, one should be aware that nonlinear price effects can occur. Such nonlinearities can be accommodated by using orthogonal polynomial codes for the linear and quadratic effects, or by using the method of Robson (1959) cited in the text. Cross-effects, which represent violations of the MNL model assumption that only the marginals matter, can be included in the model analysis by creating cross-products of a particular brand dummy with other brand-specific price effects (e.g., brand A $\times$ price of B).

Figure 4.5

bute combinations for each brand with a fractional factorial design, randomly assigning these treatments to compete with attribute combinations of other brands.

The third suggestion works because, in principle, randomization of attribute combinations between brands renders the marginals of brands independent of each other. In practice one can test the satisfaction of this condition by computing the canonical correlations for each pair of brands. If the marginals are independent, none of these correlations should be significant. Louviere (1984a, 1984b) uses this design strategy to examine the likely trial share consequences of various innovation actions that might be taken by fast-food restaurants and to study the likely pesticide choices of farmers in situations in which a set of existing chemical products compete with a newly introduced product (Louviere, 1986).

Other types of designs can be used to construct choice sets, such as incomplete block designs, Latin squares, and the like. In principle, however, one must construct two designs: one to generate attribute combinations and a second to place these combinations into choice sets. Because of their versatility and flexibility, there are many more design possibilities for choice experiments than for more traditional conjoint problems discussed in previous chapters.

An objective of applied choice studies often is to design an experiment such that it resembles real choice or shopping environments as closely as possible. Choice experiments can satisfy this objective because they easily accommodate existing brands, new product concepts, and/or nonpurchase alternatives. As well, choice experiments can be merged with marketplace choice data, paper-and-pencil choice surveys, market and product-concept tests, or other marketing data that contain choice or purchase information, such as scanner and inventory withdrawal data. Thus choice experiments can be designed to mimic real market choice situations, and can be used in connection with other marketing research data.

4.2.1.3 Individual and Segment-Level Choice Models. Unlike traditional conjoint methods, however, it is difficult to develop individual-level choice models from discrete choice experiments because one needs many more observations to attain reasonable efficiency properties (see, e.g., McFadden, 1974, or Chapman, 1984). Hence the number of observations required for problems of even modest size make individual-level analysis impractical for many applied research problems.

If one needs individual-level models, constant sum scales can be used with choice tasks if there are no more than two or three brands per choice set. In constant sum tasks subjects allocate a fixed quantity of resources (e.g., 10 points, $100, 20 chips) among the brands in each choice set. As the number of brands in a choice set increases, the number of zero allocations also increases, reducing the statistical information for model estimation. Logit and probit models seem to be reasonable descriptors of constant sum allocation data in choice tasks, but support for the applicability of these models to allocation data is lacking. Thus discrete choice models should be regarded as ad hoc descriptive techniques with unknown statistical properties for constant sum allocation data.

Cluster analysis techniques can be used to develop choice models for different segments by grouping together individuals who have similar vectors of choice responses for the same choice sets. For example, Wilkinson (1986) discusses the use of the percent matching coefficient and nearest neighbor cluster analysis for nominal data. Once mutually exclusive groups (segments) are determined, the choice data can be pooled, and dummy variables used to specify segment deviations from mean attribute effects. The within-segment attribute effects can be defined by multiplying segment member dummies with the vectors of mean attribute effects. Significant within-segment, cross-product effects indicate that segments differ from the market as a whole on those attributes.

4.3 Concluding Remarks About Choice Experiments

The approach to the design and analysis of discrete choice experiments explained in this chapter has been applied to many commercial and academic research problems, including analysis of billing and service options for new public utility and telecommunications services; forecasts of demand for new financial and transportation services, medical and pharmaceutical products, and agricultural chemicals; analysis of positioning and repositioning strategies for new and existing chemical products, political candidates, computers and retail services; and the identification of optimum packages of features, services, and options.

Understanding and predicting the choices that individuals and groups of individuals are likely to make in response to competitive actions is of major strategic and tactical interest to those who manage brands and product lines. Conjoint methods allow one to address such managerial concerns directly; and, consequently, applications of conjoint techniques to such problems has rapidly increased (Cattin and Wittink, 1982, 1986). The importance of understanding and forecasting choice behavior has encouraged the development of better approximations to consumer choice processes (see e.g., Tversky and Sattath, 1979; Rotondo, 1986; Batsell and Polking, 1985); and although other design possibilities exist, the techniques of design construction described in this monograph should permit one to study many different types of choice models and choice processes.

REFERENCES

ADELMAN, L., T. R. STEWART, and K. R. HAMMOND (1974) A Case History of the Application of Social Judgment Theory to Policy Formation. Report 173. Boulder: University of Colorado Institute of Behavioral Science.

ALPERT, M. I. (1971) "Definition of determinant attributes: a comparison of methods." J. of Marketing Research 8: 184-191.

ANDERSON, N. H. (1970) "Functional measurement and psychophysical judgment." Psych. Rev. 77: 153-170.

ANDERSON, N. H. (1971) "An exchange on functional and conjoint measurement." Psych. Rev. 78: 457-458.

ANDERSON, N. H. (1981) Foundations of Information Integration Theory. New York: Academic Press.

ANDERSON, N. H. (1982) Methods of Information Integration Theory. New York: Academic Press.

ANDERSON, N. H. and J. SHANTEAU (1977) "Weak inference with linear models." Psych. Bull. 84: 1155-1170.

BARRON, F. H. (1977) "Axiomatic conjoint measurement." Decision Sciences 8: 548-559.

BATSELL, R. R. and J. C. POLKING (1985) "A generalized model of market share." Marketing Sci. 4: 177-198.

BEN-AKIVA, M. and S. R. LERMAN (1985) Discrete Choice Analysis: Theory and Application to Travel Demand. Cambridge: MIT Press.

BETTMAN, J. R., N. CAPON, and R. J. LUTZ (1975) "Cognitive algebra in multi-attribute attitude models." J. of Marketing Research 12: 151-164.

BISHOP, Y. M. M., S. E. FIENBERG, and P. W. HOLLAND (1975) Discrete Multi-variate Analysis: Theory and Practice. Cambridge: MIT Press.

BRADLEY, M. A. and P. H. L. BOVY (1985) "Functional measurement of route choice behavior: a study of commuting cyclists in the Netherlands." Presented at the 1985 International Conference on Travel Behaviour, Noordwijk, The Netherlands, April.

CATTIN, P. and D. R. WITTINK (1982) "Commercial use of conjoint analysis: a survey." J. of Marketing 46: 44-53.

CATTIN, P. and D. R. WITTINK (1986) "Commercial use of conjoint analysis: an update." Presented at the ORSA/TIMS Marketing Science Meetings, Richardson, TX, March 12-15.

CHACKO, A. (1980) "Some investigation of fractional factorials and weighing designs." Ph.D. dissertation, University of Delhi, India.

CHAPMAN, R. G. (1984) "An approach to estimating logit models of a single decision maker's choice behavior." Advances in Consumer Research 11: 656-661.

CHURCHILL, G., Jr. (1983) Marketing Research: Methodological Foundations. Hinsdale, IL: Dryden Press.

CONNER, W. S. and M. ZELEN (1959) Fractional Factorial Experimental Designs for Factors at Three Levels. Applied Math Series S4, Washington, DC: National Bureau of Standards.

CURRY, D. J., J. J. LOUVIERE, and M. J. AUGUSTINE (1983) "The aggregate effects of induced changes in consumer decision structures." Research in Marketing 6: 65-97.

DAWES, R. M. and B. CORRIGAN (1974) "Linear models in decision making." Psych. Bull. 81: 95-106.

ELIASHBERG, J. and J. R. HAUSER (1985) "A measurement error approach for modeling consumer risk preference." Management Sci. 31: 1-25.

GESCHEIDER, G. A. (1976) Psychophysics: Method and Theory. Hillsdale, NJ: Lawrence Erlbaum.

GOLLEDGE, R. D. and TIMMERMANZ, H. (1987) Behavioural Modelling in Geography and Planning. London: Croon Helm.

GREEN, P. E. (1974) "On the design of choice experiments involving multifactor alternatives." J. of Consumer Research 1: 61-68.

GREEN, P. E., J. D. CARROLL, and S. M. GOLDBERG (1981) "A general approach to product design optimization via conjoint analysis." J. of Marketing 45: 17-37.

GREEN, P. E. and M. T. DeVITA (1974) "A complimentary model of consumer utility for item collections." J. of Consumer Research 1: 56-67.

GREEN, P. E. and V. R. RAO, (1971) "Conjoint measurement for quantifying judgmental data." J. of Marketing Research 8: 355-363.

GREEN, P. E. and V. SRINIVASAN (1978) "Conjoint analysis in consumer research: issues and outlook." J. of Consumer Research 5: 103-123.

GREEN, P. E. and D. S. TULL (1978) Research for Marketing Decisions. Englewood Cliffs, NJ: Prentice-Hall.

GREEN, P. E. and Y. WIND (1973) Multiattribute Decisions in Marketing: A Measurement Approach. Hinsdale, IL: Dryden Press.

GUILFORD, J. P. (1954) Psychometric Methods. New York: McGraw-Hill.

HAGGERTY, M. R. (1987) "The cost of simplifying preference models." Marketing Sci. 5: 298-319.

HAHN, G. J. and S. S. SHAPIRO (1966) A Catalog and Computer Program for the Design and Analysis of Orthogonal Symmetric and Assymmetric Fractional Factorial Experiments. Technical Report 66-C 165. Schenectady, NY: General Electric Research and Development Center.

HAMMOND, K. R., J. ROHRBAUGH, J. MUMPOWER, and J. ADELMAN (1977) "Social judgment theory: applications in policy formulation," in M. F. Kaplan and S. Schwartz (eds.) Human Judgment and Decision Processes in Applied Settings. New York: Academic Press.

HAYS, W. L. (1973) Statistics for the Social Sciences. New York: Holt, Rinehart & Winston.

HEDAYAT, A. and W. D. WALLIS (1978) "Hadamard matrices and their applications." Annals of Statistics 6: 1184-1238.

HENSHER, D. A. and L. JOHNSON (1980) Applied Discrete Choice Modeling. London: Croom-Helm.

KEENEY, R. L. and H. RAIFFA (1976) Decisions with Multiple Objectives: Preferences and Value Tradeoffs. New York: John Wiley.

KELLY, G. A. (1955) Psychology of Personal Constructs. New York: W. W. Norton.

KINNEAR, T. C. and J. R. TAYLOR (1983) Marketing Research: An Applied Approach. New York: McGraw-Hill.

KOCUR, G., W. HYMAN, and B. AUNET (1982) "Wisconsin work mode-choice models based on functional measurement and disaggregate behavioral data." Transportation Research Record 895: 24-31.

KRANTZ, D. H., R. D. LUCE, P. SUPPES, and A. TVERSKY (1971) Foundations of Measurement. New York: Academic Press.

KRANTZ, D. H. and A. TVERSKY (1971b) "Conjoint-measurement analysis of composition rules in psychology." Psych. Rev. 78: 151-169.

KRANTZ, D. H. and A. TVERSKY (1971a) "An exchange on functional and conjoint measurement." Psych. Rev. 78: 457-458.

KRUSKAL, J. B. (1965) "Analysis of factorial experiments by estimating monotone transformations of the data." J. of the Royal Stat. Society, Series B 27: 251-263.

LAVIDGE, R. J. and G. A. STEINER (1961) "A model for predictive measurements of advertising effectiveness." J. of Marketing 25: 59-62.

LEHMANN, D. R. (1985) Market Research and Analysis. Homewood, IL: Richard D. Irwin.

LERMAN, S. R. and J. J. LOUVIERE (1978) "On the use of direct utility assessment to identify the functional form of utility and destination choice models." Transportation Research Record 673: 78-86.

LEVIN, I. P. and R. D. HERRING (1981) "Functional measurement of qualitative variables in mode choice: ratings of economy, safety and desirability of flying versus driving." Transportation Research 15A: 207-214.

LEVIN, I. P., J. J. LOUVIERE, A. A. SCHEPANSKI, and K. L. NORMAN (1983) "External validity tests of laboratory studies of information integration." Organizational Behavior and Human Performance 31: 173-193.

LOPES, L. L. (1986) "Between hope and fear: the psychology of risk." Presented at the Behavioral Decision Theory Seminar, Faculty of Business, University of Alberta, Edmonton, April.

LOUVIERE, J. J. (1974) "Predicting the evaluation of real stimulus objects from an abstract evaluation of their attributes: the case of trout streams." J. of Applied Psychology 59, 5: 572-577.

LOUVIERE, J. J. (1979) "Modeling individual residential preferences: a totally disaggregate approach." Transportation Research 13A: 374-384.

LOUVIERE, J. J. (1982) Analysis of Housing Choices of the Elderly. Technical Report 138, Institute of Urban and Regional Research, University of Iowa, Iowa City.

LOUVIERE, J. J. (1983) "Integrating conjoint and functional measurement with discrete choice theory: an experimental design approach." Advances in Consumer Research 10: 151-156.

LOUVIERE, J. J. (1984a) "Hierarchical information integration: a new method for the design and analysis of complex multiattribute judgment problems." Advances in Consumer Research 11: 148-155.

LOUVIERE, J. J. (1984b) "Using discrete choice experiments and multinomial logit choice models to forecast trial in a competitive retail environment: a fast food restaurant illustration." J. of Retailing 60: 81-107.

LOUVIERE, J. J. (1986) "A conjoint model for analyzing new product positions in a differentiated market with price competition." Advances in Consumer Research 13: 375-380.

LOUVIERE, J. J. (1988) "An experimental design approach to the development of conjoint based choice simulation systems with an application to forecasting future retirement choices," in R.J.G. Golledge and H. G. Timmermans (eds.) Behavioral Modeling in Geography and Planning. London: Croom-Helm.

LOUVIERE, J. J., L. L. BEAVERS, K. L. NORMAN, and F. STETZER (1973) Theory, Methodology and Findings in Mode Choice Behavior. Working Paper 11, Institute of Urban and Regional Research, University of Iowa, Iowa City.

— LOUVIERE, J. J., D. H. HENLEY, G. WOODWORTH, R. J. MEYER, I. P. LEVIN, J. W. STONER, D. CURRY, and D. A. ANDERSON (1981) "Laboratory simulation versus revealed preference methods for estimating travel demand models: an empirical comparison." Transportation Research Record, 79: 42-51.

LOUVIERE, J. J. and D. A. HENSHER (1982) "On the design and analysis of simulated choice or allocation experiments in travel choice modeling." Transportation Research Record 890: 11-17.

— LOUVIERE, J. J. and D. A. HENSHER (1983) "Using discrete choice models with experimental design data to forecast consumer demand for a unique cultural event." J. of Consumer Research 10: 348-361.

LOUVIERE, J. J. and G. KOCUR (1983) "The magnitude of individual level variations in demand coefficients: a Xenia, Ohio, case example." Transportation Research, 890:11-17.

LOUVIERE, J. J. and R. J. MEYER (1981) "A composite attitude-behavior model of traveller decision making." Transportation Research 158, 5: 411-420.

LOUVIERE, J. J., R. J. MEYER, F. STETZER, and L. L. BEAVERS (1974) Application of Fractional Factorial Experiments to Bus Mode Choice Decision Making. Technical Report, Institute of Urban and Regional Research, University of Iowa, Iowa City.

LOUVIERE, J. J. and M. PICCOLO (1977) "Information integration theory applied to real-world choice behavior: validation experiments involving out of-town shopping and residential choice." Special issue of Great Plains/Rocky Mountains Geographical J., 6: 5-21.

— LOUVIERE, J. J. and G. G. WOODWORTH (1983) "Design and analysis of simulated consumer choice or allocation experiments: an approach based on aggregate data." J. of Marketing Research 20: 350-367.

LUCE, R. D. (1959) Individual Choice Behavior. New York: John Wiley.

LUCE, R. D. (1977) "The Choice Axiom After Twenty Years." J. of Mathematical Psychology 3: 215-233.

LUCE, R. D. (1981) "Axioms for the averaging and adding representations of functional measurement." Mathematical Social Sciences 1: 139-144.

LUCE, R. D. and J. W. TUKEY (1964) "Simultaneous conjoint measurement: a new type of fundamental measurement." J. of Mathematical Psychology 1: 1-27.

LUTZ, R. J. (1975) "Changing brand attitudes through modification of cognitive structures." J. of Consumer Research 1: 49-59.

LYNCH, J. G. (1985) "Uniqueness issues in the decompositional modeling of multi-attribute overall evaluations." J. of Marketing Research 22: 1-19.

MADDALA, G. S. (1983) Limited Dependent and Qualitative Variables in Econometrics. New York: Cambridge University Press.

MAHAJAN, V., T. E. GREEN, and S. M. GOLDBERG (1982) "A conjoint model for measuring self- and cross-price/demand relationships." J. of Marketing Research, 19: 334-342.

MALHOTRA, N. K. (1983) "A threshold model of store choice." J. of Retailing 59, 2: 3-21.

MANSKI, C. F. and D. MCFADDEN (1981) Structural Analysis of Discrete Data with Econometric Applications. Cambridge: MIT Press.

McCLELLAND, G. H. (1979) A Psychological and Measurement Theory Approach to Fertility Decision Making. Report 219, Institute of Behavioral Science, Center for Research on Judgment and Policy, University of Colorado, Boulder.

McCLELLAND, G. H. (1980) Axioms for the Weighted Linear Model. Report 227, Institute of Behavioral Science, Center for Research on Judgment and Policy, University of Colorado, Boulder.

McFADDEN, D. (1974) "Conditional logit analysis of qualitative choice behavior," pp. 105-142 in P. Zarembka (ed.) Frontiers in Econometrics. New York: Academic Press.

McFADDEN, D. (1981) "Econometric models of probabilistic choice," pp. 198-272 in C. F. Manski and D. McFadden (1981) Structural Analysis of Discrete Data with Econometric Applications. Cambridge: MIT Press.

McLEAN, R. and V. ANDERSON (1984) Applied Factorial and Fractional Designs. New York: Marcel Deckker.

MEYER, R. J. (1977) "An experimental analysis of student apartment selection decisions under uncertainty." Special issue on human judgment and spatial behavior Great Plains-Rocky Mountains Geographical J. 6: 30-38.

MEYER, R. J., I. P. LEVIN, and J. J. LOUVIERE (1978) "Functional analysis of mode choice." Transportation Research Record 673: 1-7.

MILLER, D. C. (1983) Handbook of Research Design and Social Measurement. New York: Longman.

MYERS, J. H. and A. D. SHOCKER (1981) "The nature of product-related attributes," pp. 211-236 in J. N. Sheth (ed.) Research in Marketing, Vol. 4. Greenwich, TN: JAI Press.

NAKANISHI, M. and L. G. COOPER (1982) "Simplified estimation procedure for MCI models." Marketing Sci. 1, 3: 314-322.

NORMAN, K. L. (1977) "Attributes in bus transportation: importance depends on trip purpose." J. of Applied Psychology 62: 164-170.

NORMAN, K. L. and J. J. LOUVIERE (1974) "Integration of attributes in public bus transportation: two modeling approaches." J. of Applied Psychology 59: 753-758.

PERREAULT, W. D. and H. C. BARKSDALE (1980) "A model-free approach for analysis of complex contingency data in survey research." J. of Marketing Research 17: 503-515.

ROBSON, D. S. (1959) "A simple method for constructing orthogonal polynomials when the independent variable is unequally spaced." Biometrics 15: 187-191.

ROTONDO, J. (1986) "Price as an aspect of choice in EBA." Marketing Sci. 5: 391-402. ⟵

SLOVIC, P. and S. LICHTENSTEIN (1971) "Comparison of Bayesian and regression approaches to the study of information processing in judgment." Organizational Behavior and Human Performance 6: 649-744.

SLOVIC, P., B. FISCHHOFF, and S. J. LICHTENSTEIN (1977) "Behavioral decision theory." Annual Rev. of Psychology 28: 1-39.

SNEDECOR, G. W. and W. G. COCHRAN (1974) Statistical Methods. Ames: Iowa State University Press.

THURSTONE, L. L. (1927) "A law of comparative judgment." Psych. Rev. 34: 273-286.

TIMMERMANS, H. G. (1982) "Consumer choice of shopping centre: an information integration approach." Regional Studies 16, 3: 171-182.

TVERSKY, A. (1967) "A general theory of polynomial conjoint measurement." J. of Mathematical Psychology 4:1-20.

TVERSKY, A. and S. SATTATH (1979) "Preference trees." Psych. Rev. 86: 542-573.

URBAN, G. L. and J. R. HAUSER (1980) Design and Marketing of New Products. Englewood Cliffs, NJ: Prentice-Hall.

WILKINSON, L. (1986) SYSTAT: The System for Statistics (1984). Evanston, IL: SYSTAT.

WINER, B. J. (1971) Statistical Principles in Experimental Design. New York: McGraw-Hill.

WOODWORTH, G. G. and J. J. LOUVIERE (1984) "An approach to estimating the parameters of large multinomial logit models." Presented at the ORSA/TIMS Marketing Science Meetings, Nashville, TN, March.

ABOUT THE AUTHOR

JORDAN J. LOUVIERE *is Professor of Marketing and Economic Analysis at the University of Alberta. He has taught courses in modeling consumer behavior and consumer information processing, and the relationship of consumer choice behavior to managerial decision making and the objectives of organizations at Florida State University, the University of Wyoming, the University of Iowa, the Australian Graduate School of Management, and the University of Alberta. His major research area is the design and analysis of discrete dependent variable experiments and data collection efforts related to understanding and predicting consumer decision making and choice behavior. He has published numerous theoretical, methodological, and empirical articles in scholarly journals on consumer decision making in marketing and transportation planning, including* Journal of Consumer Research, Journal of Marketing Research, Journal of Retailing, Transportation Research, *and* Journal of Applied Psychology.

NOTES

Quantitative Applications in the Social Sciences

(a Sage University Papers Series)

$6.00 each

Place
Stamp
here

SAGE PUBLICATIONS, INC.
P.O. BOX 5084
NEWBURY PARK, CALIFORNIA 91359—9924